Books are to be returned

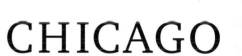

CHICAGO

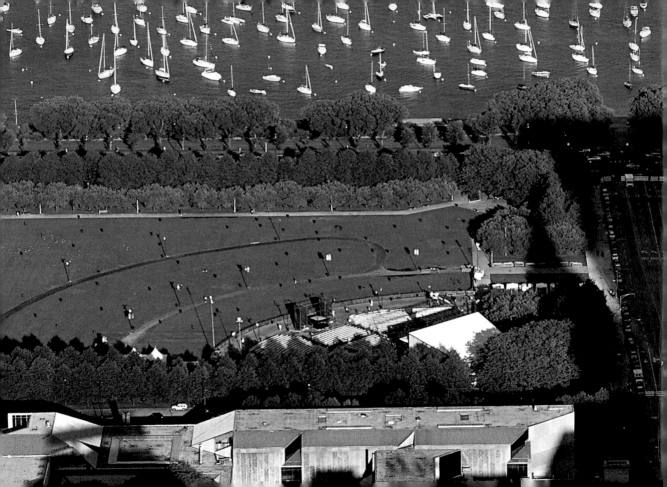

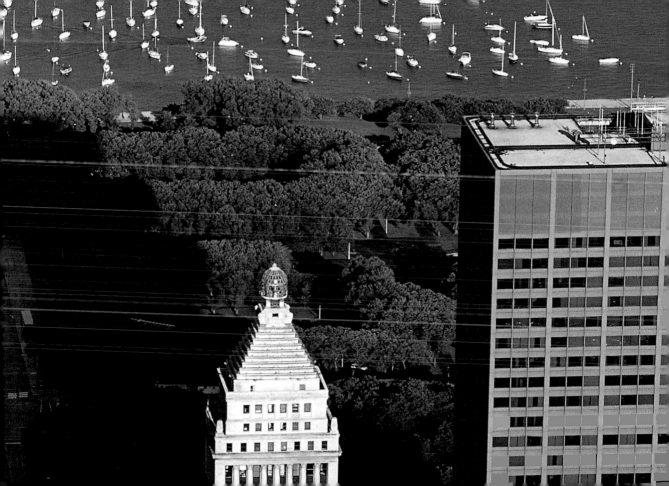

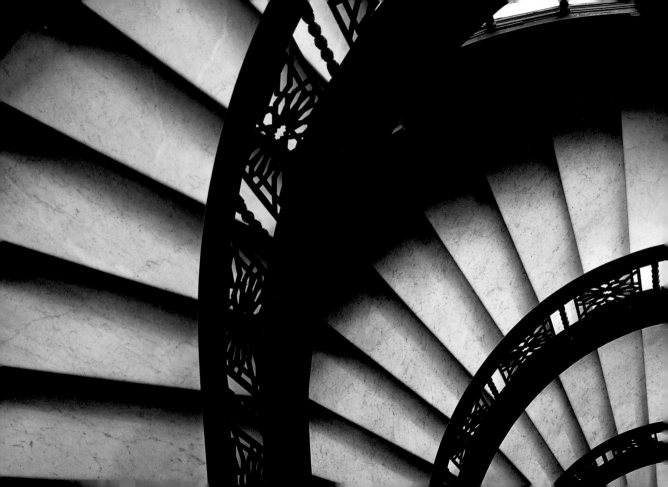

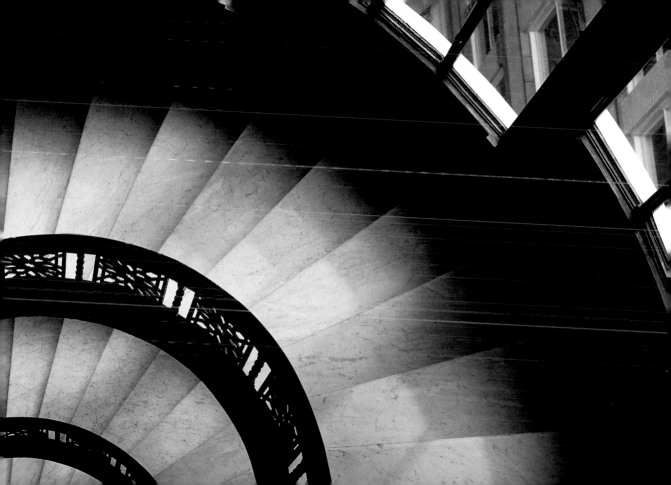

CHIC

CAGO

PHOTOGRAPHS BY SANTI VISALLI / INTRODUCTION BY STANLEY TIGERMAN

Rizzoli

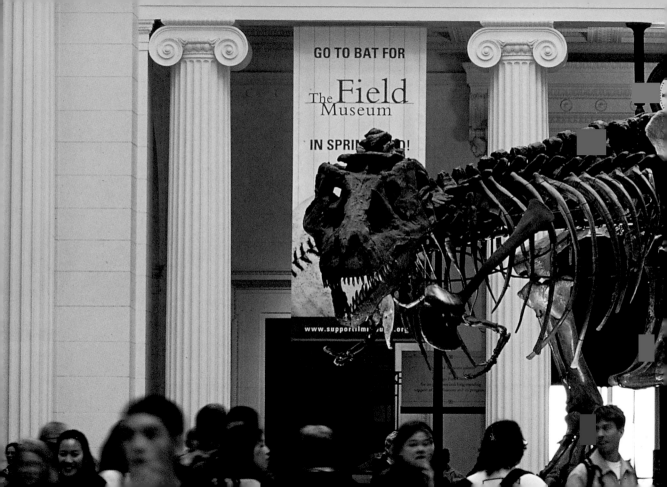

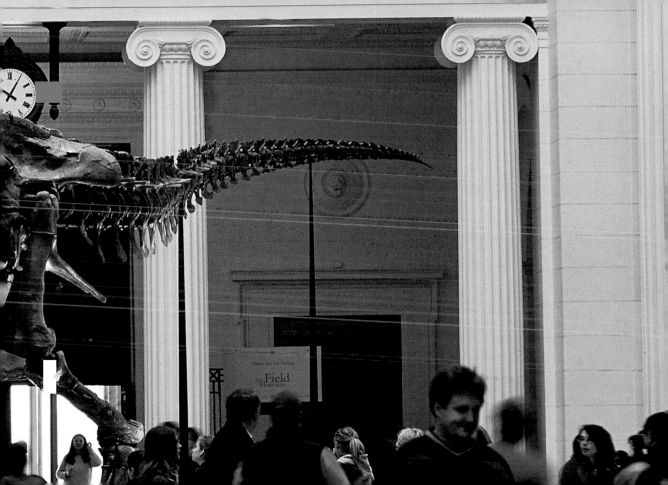

First published in the United States of
America in 2005
by Rizzoli International Publications
300 Park Avenue South
New York, NY 10010
www.rizzoliusa.com

© 2004 Santi Visalli
Introduction by Stanley Tigerman

2005 2006 2007 2008 / 10 9 8 7 6 5 4 3 2 1

Design by Opto Design

Printed in China

ISBN: 0–8478–2709–7

Library of Congress Control Number:
2004095072

Opposite: Skyline at dawn, viewed from
the Max Adler Planetarium

ACKNOWLEDGMENTS
This book would never have been
possible without the cooperation of
many people in Chicago, who are very
proud of their beautiful city, and rightly
so. I especially want to thank Mayor
Richard M. Daley, who has been
instrumental in transforming the City
on the Lake. Also, my wife, Gayla, who
never complained about getting up at
five in the morning to photograph a
sunrise or a hotel lobby or working
sixteen-hour days. And Michael
Jungert, my agent and sometime assis-
tant, who managed to fit my needs in
with his own work for TIPS Chicago.
Also my two assistants, Jessa Chin and
Kathy Carey, who put in long, hectic,
and sometimes frustrating hours.

Some of the spectacular views from
aloft were made possible by Mark
Spencer, who managed to get me into
strategic places in the Sears Tower.

And Denis Nervig of Fuji Film loaned
me the Fuji large-format GX-17
panorama camera, with which I took
the gatefold shots.

I thank Cheryl A. Bachand of the
Frank Lloyd Wright Preservation Trust
for permission to photograph the
Frederick C. Robie House in Chicago
and the Frank Lloyd Wright Studio and
Home in Oak Park; Esther M. Robson
for allowing me to photograph the mag-
nificent swimming pool at the Intercon-
tinental Hotel; and Jane and Roger
Tracy and Biba and Peter Roesch, who
helped me with numerous introductions
and suggestions for locations.

These people were also especially
helpful: Rick Myers (Illinois Institute
of Technology); Jack Zimmerman and
Michael Kuropas (the Civic Opera);
Emmanuel Nony and Jennifer Chen
(NoMi Restaurant at the Park Hyatt
Hotel); John Holden (the Chicago
Mercantile Exchange); Chai Lee (the
Art Institute of Chicago); Jeannine M.
Rio (the beautifully restored Rookery);
Laurence Hill, Larry Arbeiter, Cinthia
Bold (the University of Chicago);

Barnaby Dinges (Soldier Field); Nancy
O'Shea (the Field Museum); Eileen
Locario and Lauren Klein (the Ford
Center); Judy Green (the Auditorium);
and Eva Penar (the Mexican Fine Art
Museum Center).

For their generous hospitality
during my several trips to Chicago I
thank Ellen Cho of the Drake Hotel;
"the host of Chicago," Ken Price, of
the Palmer House; and Julia Robinson,
Director of Publications at the
University of Chicago. And these people were steadfast supporters: my pub-
lisher, Charles Miers; my hard-working
and patient editor, Holly Rothman; and
the book's talented designers, John
Klotnia and his team at Opto Design.

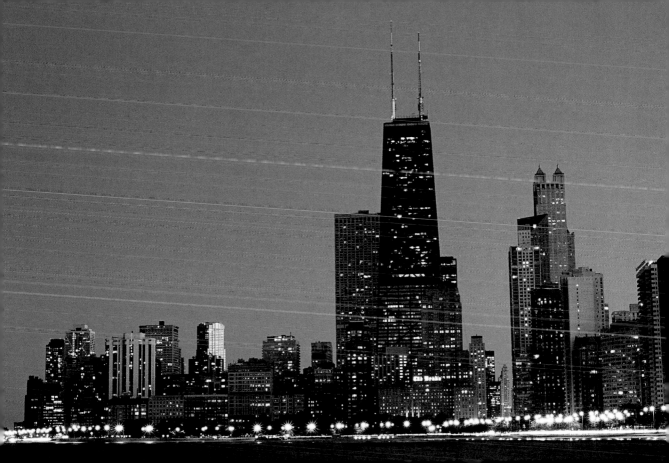

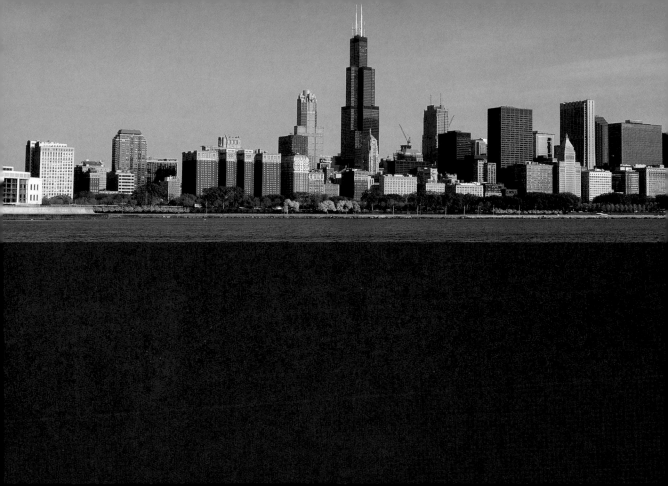

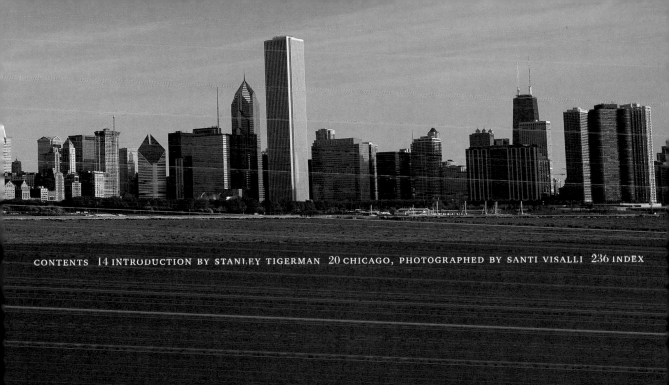

CHICAGO ARCHITECTURE (THEN AND NOW)

CHICAGO'S HISTORY AS OBSERVED (simplistically, yet importantly) by its cabbies, has alternately benefited from and been burdened by: the Native American origin of its name ("Chicagou" means "smelly onion"); the infamous—made famous by Upton Sinclair—Stock Yards; Al "Scarface" Capone; a substantial middle-European blue-collar working class (not particularly noted for its tolerance of others); unpredictable (but almost always marginal) professional sports teams; and lastly, modern architecture (with a Capital "A!"). At some level, the etymology of the final category can be largely attributed to the 1871 inferno that virtually destroyed the city's Central Business District. Consequently, Chicago had to rebuild instantaneously so as to keep the city both commercially viable and competitive with other emerging American "power places."

Two conditions came about as a result of the heroic struggle to raise our modern Midwest metropolis. The first big change was that modern technology was for the first time exploited as much as it could be, from the use of cast iron structural framing to the electric elevator. Less tangible was the phoenix that emerged from this latter-nineteenth century conflagration: The now-famous Chicago "I will!" spirit kicked into overdrive.

ONLY (MUCH) LATER DID ARCHITECTURAL HISTORIANS and the general public come to understand—and then to belatedly elevate—what at first seemed to be building expediently to the level of architecture-as-art. Then, and only then, did Chicago come to be known as the most modern city on earth.

Imagine, if you will, a man-made oasis situated on the seam separating an inland sea from an endless prairie. Now imagine the Jeffersonian one hundred x one hundred meter gridiron plan tilted up into space *après le deluge* as a three-dimensional constructional matrix: Voila, you now understand the structural—and more importantly, the visual—authority that the "First Chicago School of Architecture" superposed upon Chicago!

Ten of Chicago's nineteenth-century architectural forerunners were particularly legendary, even in their own time: Daniel

Burnham, Henry Ives Cobb, William Holabird, William Le Baron Jenney, Dwight Perkins, Martin Roche, John Wellborn Root, Howard van Doren Shaw, Louis Henri Sullivan, and Frank Lloyd Wright. Almost a half century later, the eleventh and perhaps most seminal architect, Ludwig Mies van der Rohe, arrived on our shores. It would be in his name that the so-called "Second Chicago School" would come into being.

With the exception of Shaw, none were native to Chicago, but all understood that to be an architect in Chicago was like having the provenance of being a Muslim in Mecca. They also seemed to understand the open-ended opportunities offered to those who would stake their future on a city whose indeterminacy was its most overarching characteristic.

JUST TO PLUCK TWO NAMES from this Pantheon of architectural giants: Frank Lloyd Wright and Mies van der Rohe. As the "Mister Chips" of architectural history, Vincent Scully once observed (sarcastically as Easterners are wont to do): "Frank Lloyd Wright was the greatest architect of the nineteenth century." If that was indeed the case, then for many of us, Mies van der Rohe was arguably the greatest architect of the twentieth century. Wright himself left behind more than fifty houses in greater Chicago, while Mies authored forty-five buildings conceived and built during the (final) thirty-two years of his life here. Clearly, Chicago was a privileged city: Wright and Mies produced more in Chicago than in any other locale.

Lesser—but not so lesser—architectural luminaries have worked in Chicago throughout time, but they needn't be mentioned here simply to prove the city's singular reputation historically as the world's primary modern architectural Mecca. The preponderance of so many jewels in the city's architectural crown has fed upon itself through the many generations since the Great Fire: These architects seek simply to keep up with the high level of quality that their predecessors left behind, that they laid down as a gauntlet.

But it is not only the tall building (the skyscraper, the high-rise) upon which Chicago's preeminent architectural reputation resides. The "prairie school" that Frank Lloyd Wright initiated was followed by his many talented successors whose domestic work influenced several generations of architects throughout the United States. The open kitchen, the corner window, the cantilevered roof, the wing wall– all of these innovations influenced (for better and for worse) suburban tract housing countrywide.

THE ABSENCE OF COMPETING LANDFORMS, like hills and dales, mountains, and forested topologies, has allowed for a kind of Tabula Rasa for Chicago's architects. In the end, the broad sweep of both lake and prairie seem continuously fresh as a daisy, apparently just waiting for man-made new forms to make a mark. Think of "the machine in the garden," something that architects at their most poetic can accomplish, at least from a dialectical point of view.

There is something else that is uniquely optimistic about Chicago's open-ended brand of architecture and the way it relates to how our city's population presents itself to those new to the "Capital of Middle America." The perception begins with the gridiron plan of the city itself. That Cartesian grid is open, democratic, and yet, in equal terms, alienating. Unlike European hierarchically disposed street patterns that favor either the Church and/or the Town Square, only to quickly fade to residential "*Quartier(s)*," Chicago's undifferentiated ground plan refers to the optimistic, multivalent inclusion that is uniquely representative of American democracy.

THE CITY'S RESULTING ARCHITECTURE is equally open-ended and non-hierarchical. Chicago is, in many ways, our most American city. Not excessively representative of either European, Asian, African, or Latin influence, and geographically far enough from our coastlines to be perceivably detached from them, ours is the ultimate example of a hybridized amalgam of many cultures. The architecture of the American heartland may have nothing about it that emanates directly from history, but its originality is precisely that– a hybridization of every prior precedent, which seems to constitute an original.

Multiple linguistic readings of architectural form are available here for continuous interpretation by all: For every European basilica, in America's heartland it is transmuted into a barn, just as Europe's many *campanile* become silos. Nowhere else in America do images get more blurred from the religious to the vernacular than in our farm country—and Chicago is the capital of those American values freed from historic influence.

Of course, there is a bit of a dark side to all of this as well. The same shimmering oasis that visitors flying into the city perceive through the clouds also happens to be situated in the virtual geographical center of an apparently conservative—some think fundamentalist—farm country. In that sense, it always amazes me just how open Chicagoans are to new architectural forms. Visiting architects are always startled by Chicago's brand of architectural Valhalla—both quantitatively and qualitatively. They wonder how a not-particularly intellectual center can be so supportive of an amazing level of innovation. But that's just it! It is because we are not overly burdened by the notorious "Eastern intellectual foreplay" that we are able to work unfettered by unnecessary verbal rationalizations of the nature of our architectural production.

AND THEN THERE IS OUR LESS-THAN-WELCOMING CLIMATE. It is said that the severity of Chicago's winters are such that "one can only make babies or buildings" during that bleak time of year. From an urbanistically spatial point of view, Chicago is a bit like Goldilocks: Where New York's skyscrapers seem to be oppressively close together for their height, and Los Angeles's a bit too far apart to even define the street, Chicago's Central Business District high-rises seem to be "just right."

On the other hand, Chicago's low-rise housing stock is something like Melbourne, Australia's, in that the "bungalow" in both cases produces a context that is, domestically speaking, welcoming. Chicago's recent low-rise housing developments are a bit more compressed then the detached housing that evolved a century ago, but they preserve the inviting sense of neighborhood, while being only slightly more dense than their predecessor's domestic typology.

BUT CHICAGO IS NOT ONLY ABOUT "CONTEXT" in the most polite sense of the word. Increasingly, the idiosyncratic one-off building appears on the scene as a refreshing change to what would otherwise be frankly boring as hell. Case in point: the less-than-scintillating high-rise condominium craze is more than once refreshingly disrupted by delightful experiments in multi-family living high above street level, proving that Chicago's newest generation of architects is not intimidated by precedent, good or bad.

Which brings me to that newest architectural generation itself. The element that most influenced our youngest architects to be formally, structurally, constructionally, and contextually free from the past, came about in part as a result of breaking the stranglehold that our own one-dimensional reputation provided—both here as well as abroad. Both Chicago Schools of Architecture have now been, happily or less so, relegated to history. Of course, we respect our brilliant but often one-dimensional past (and their authors, naturally, as well); but we are free of them at last. Their dominance, and more than occasionally, their preservation, both in education as well as in practice, is over. The resulting freedom represents another kind of Tabula Rasa that now establishes an open-ended set of circumstances that welcomes young architects to our shores as never before.

WORDS ABOUT THE ARCHITECTURAL WONDERS of Chicago is but one way to engage this amazing city. There is, however, no doubt that visualizations are genuinely significant in tantalizing strangers to these shores about what (if they are lucky) they may come to know should they happen to not overfly Chicago on their way to and from America's coastlines.

So now comes this exquisite photographic document of many seminal structures (and some interiors as well) authored by many of the above-listed legendary architects, together with the work of their descendants (both sycophantic AND rebellious). Comparisons will no doubt abound: suffice it to say that architecture is alive and well, and at home in Chicago.

Stanley Tigerman
Chicago, March 2004

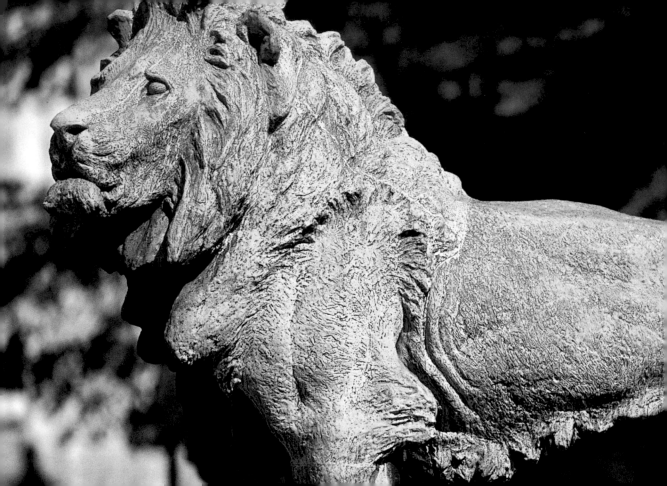

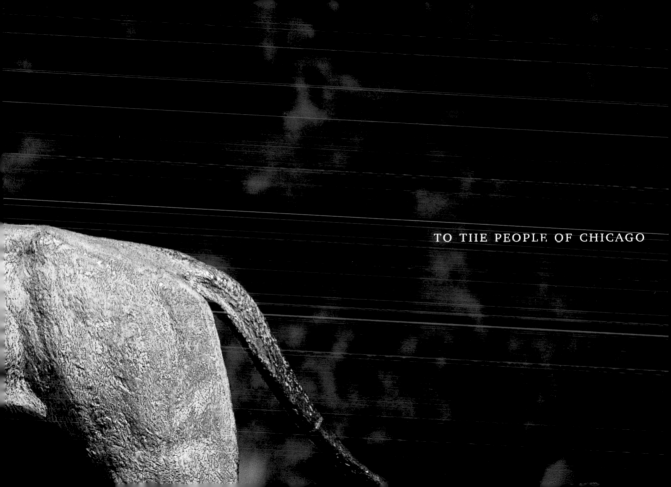

TO THE PEOPLE OF CHICAGO

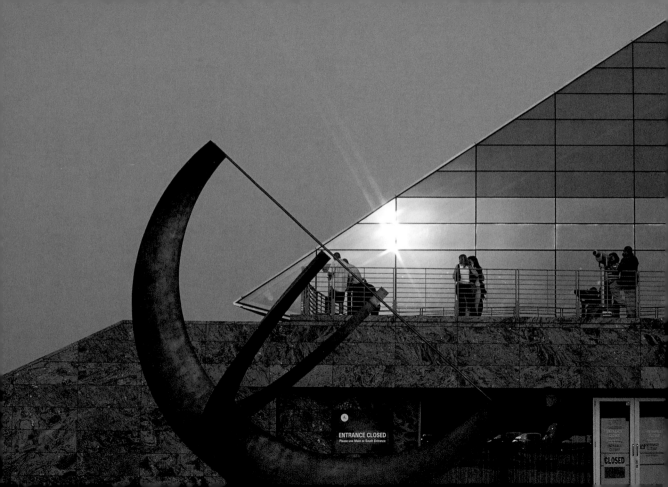

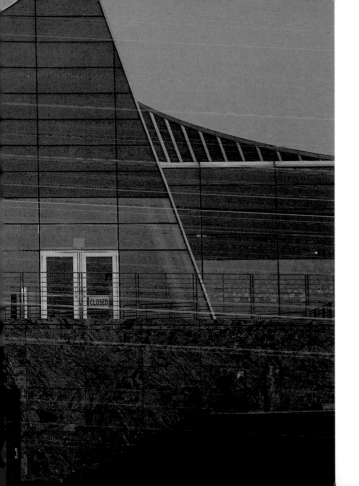

24

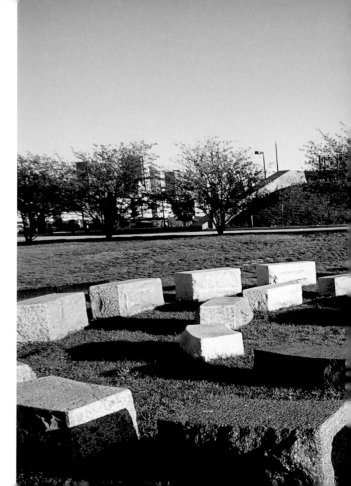

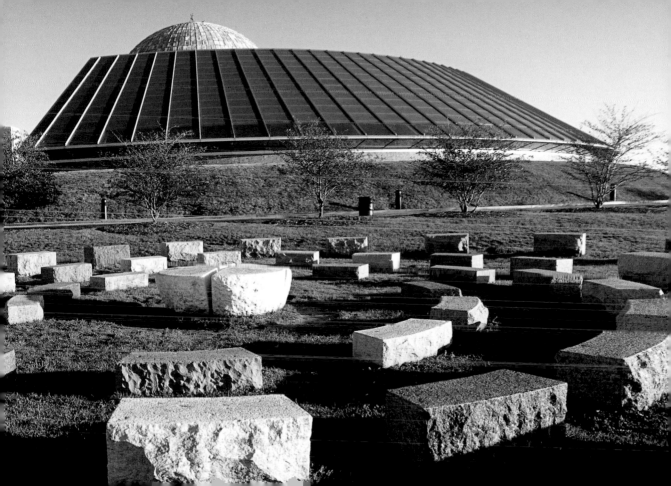

26

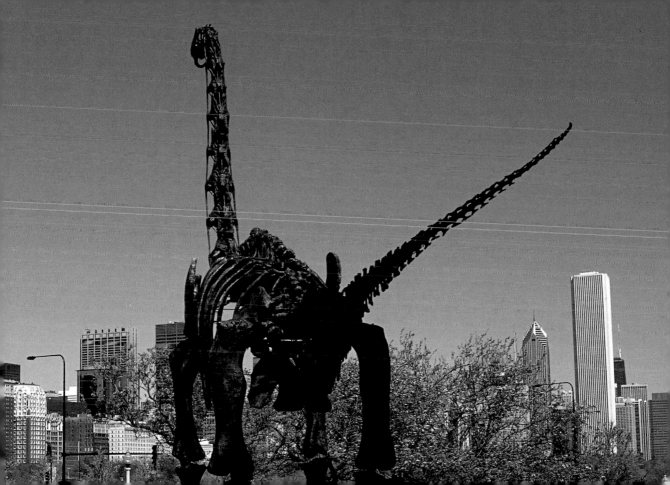

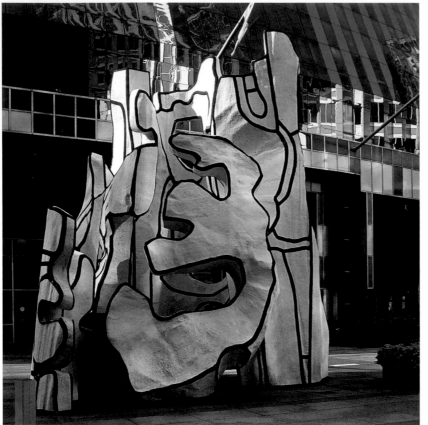

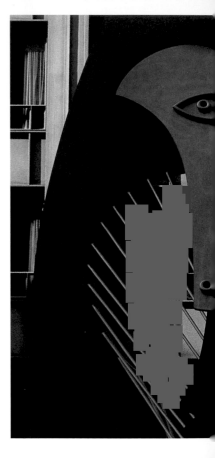

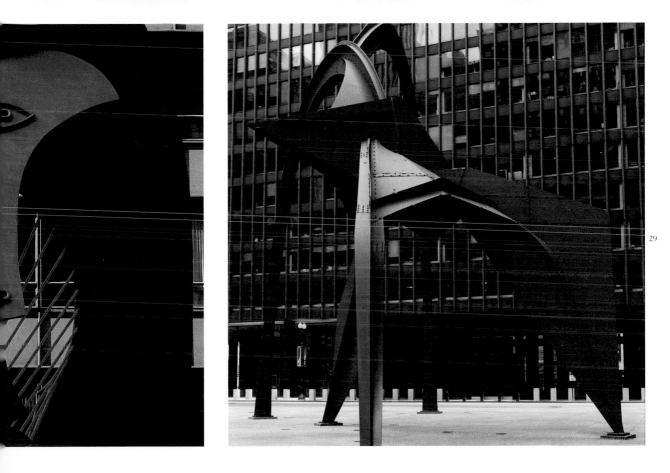

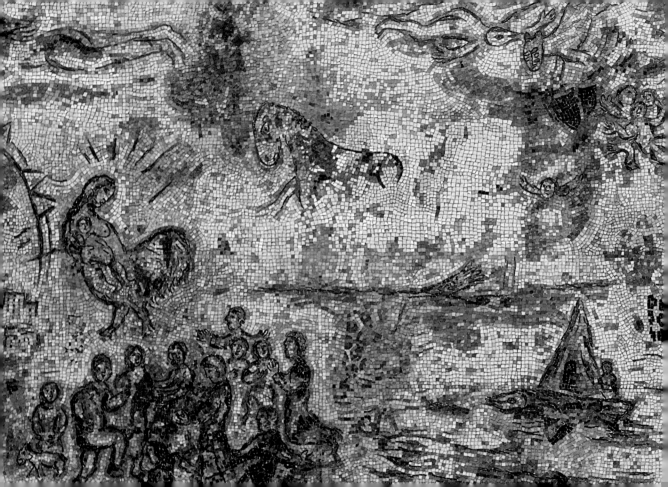

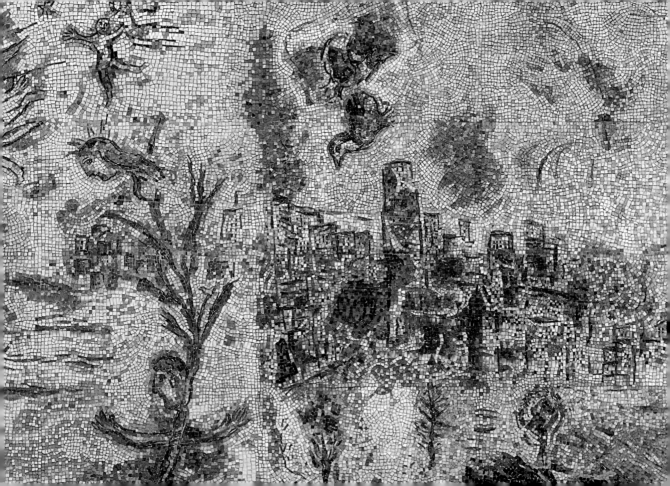

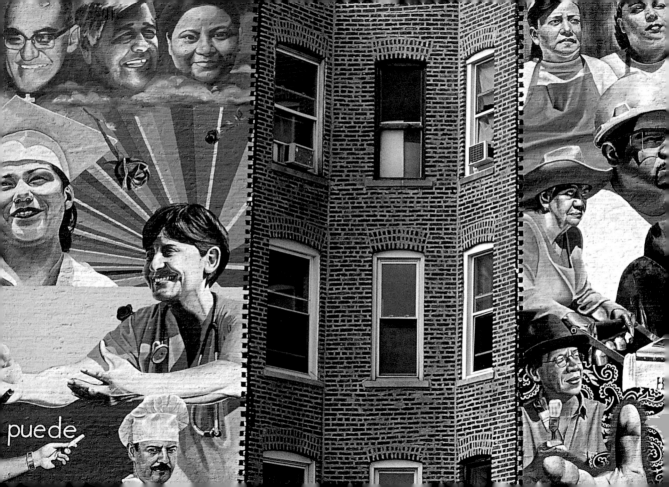

puede

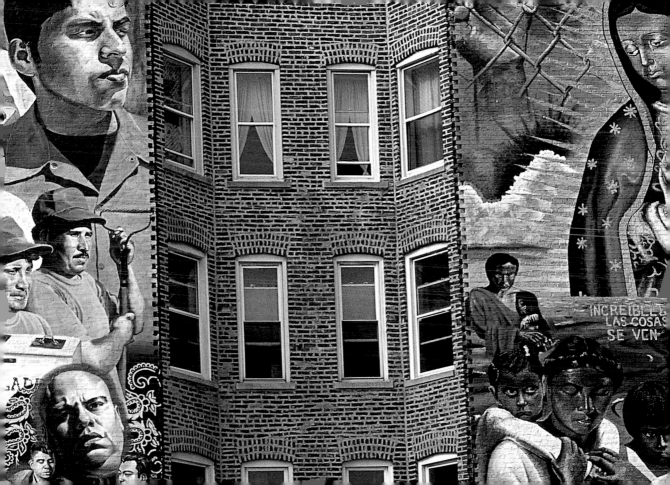

INCREIBLE
LAS COSAS
SE VEN

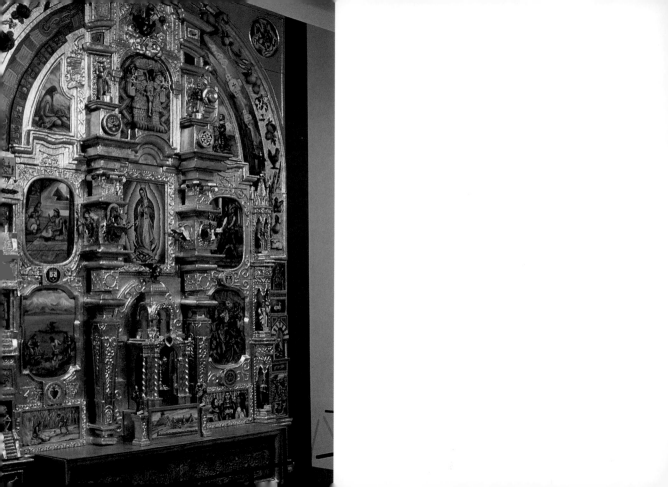

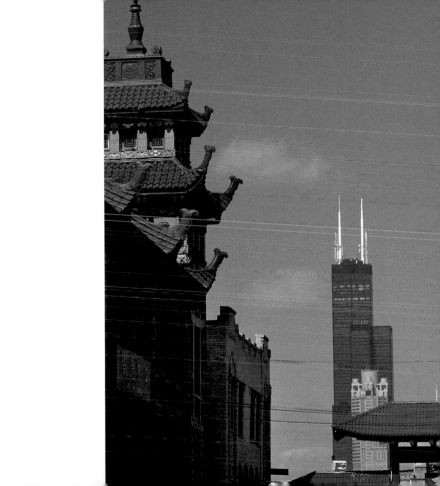

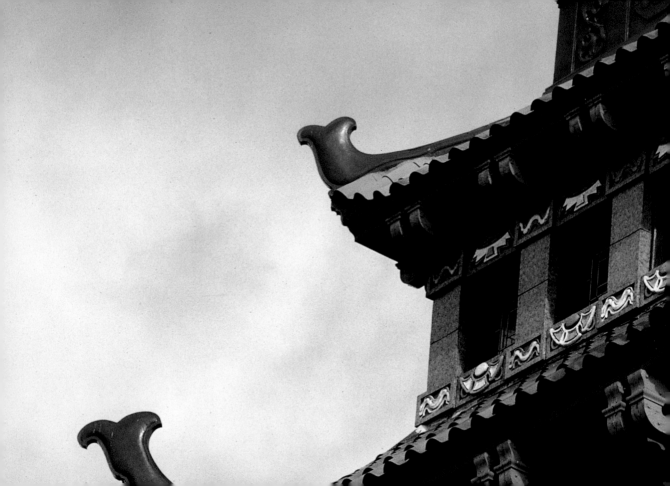

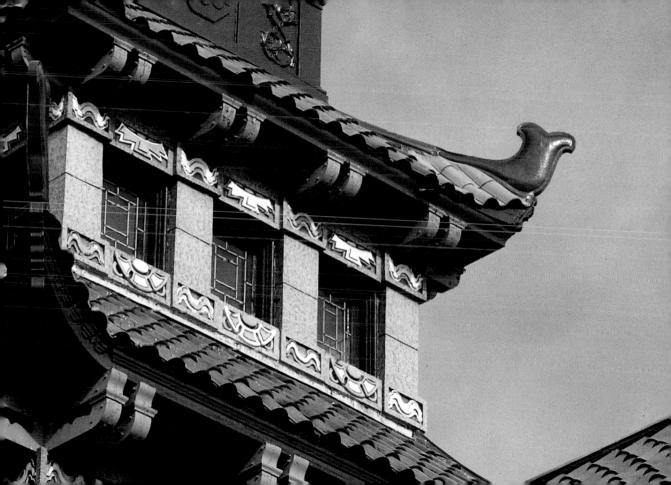

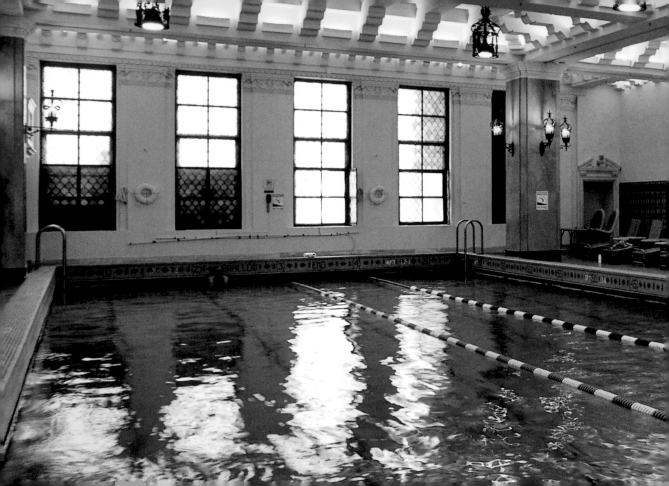

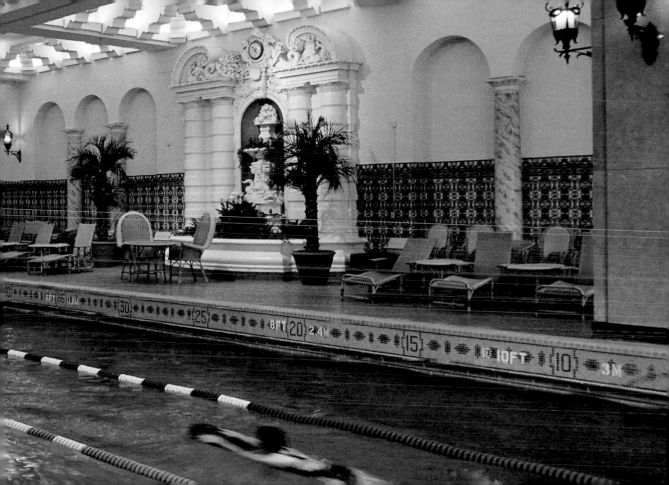

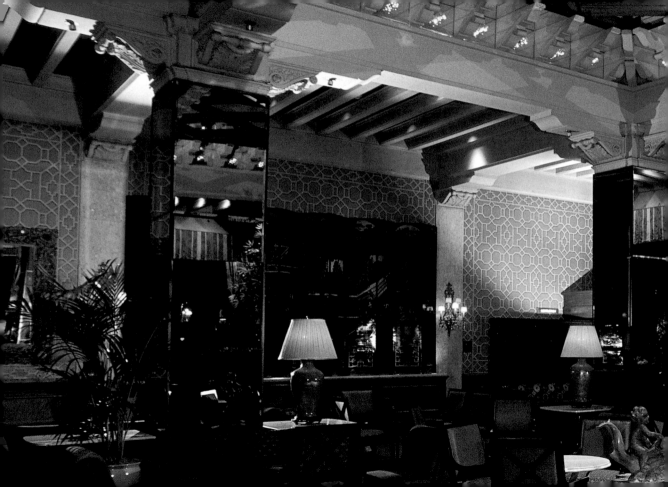

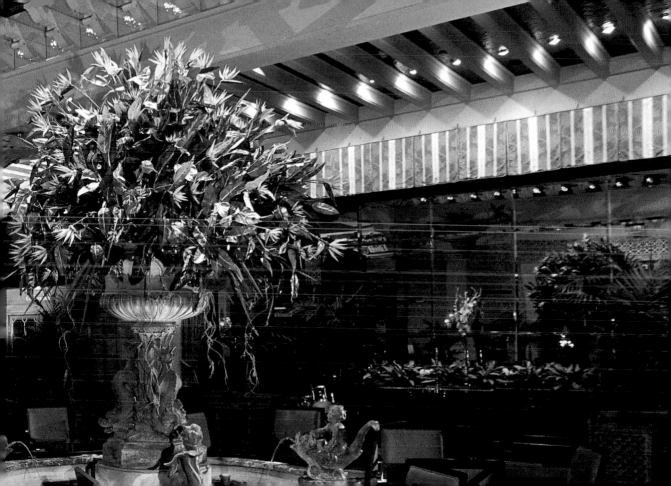

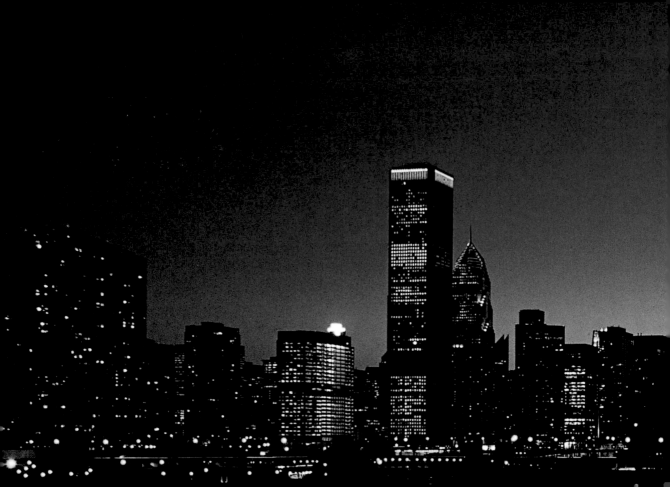

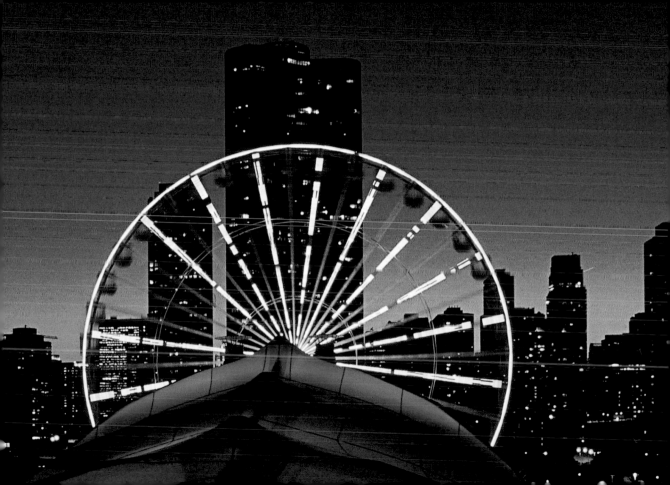

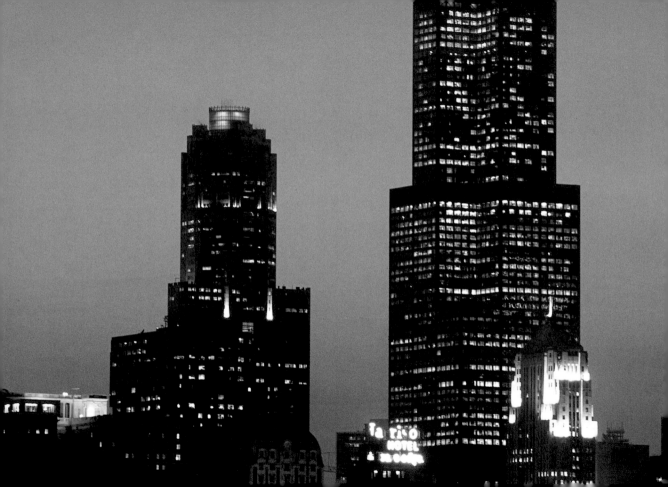

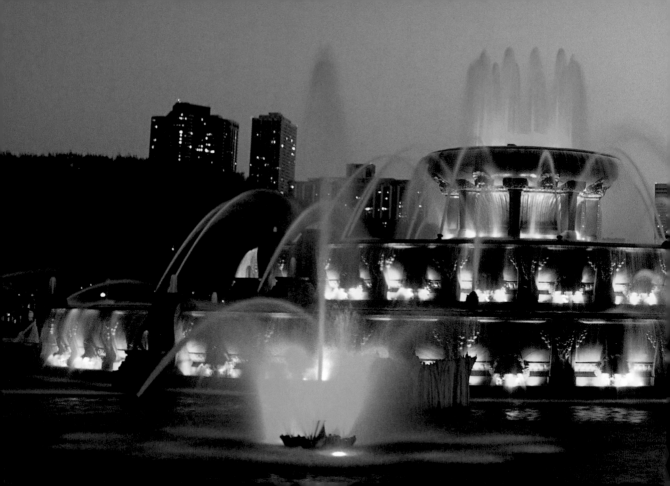

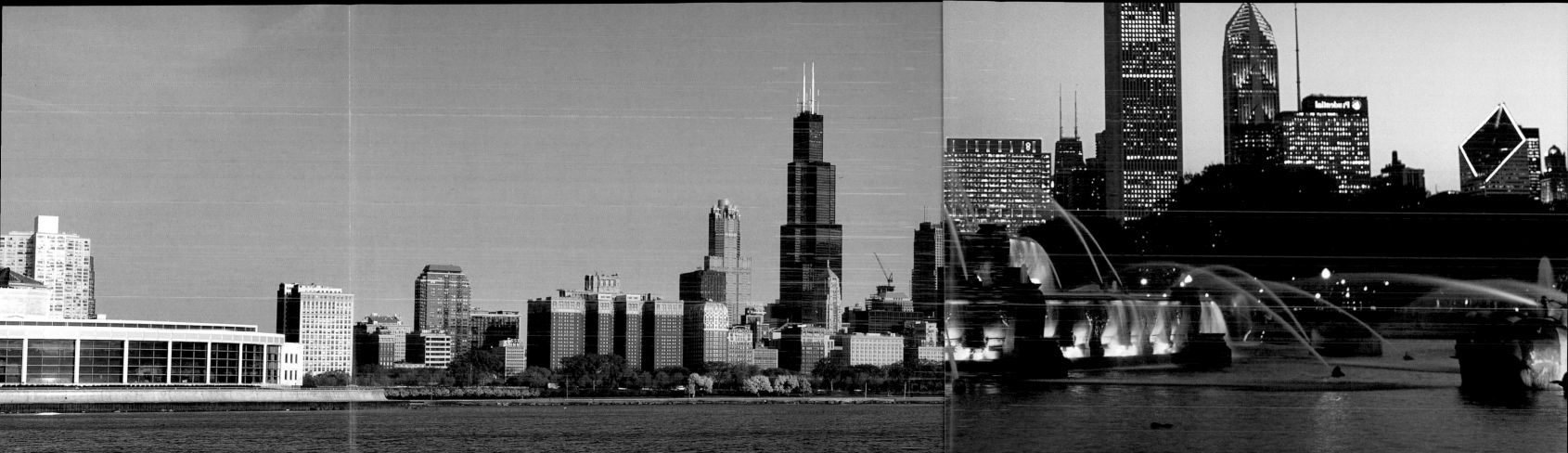

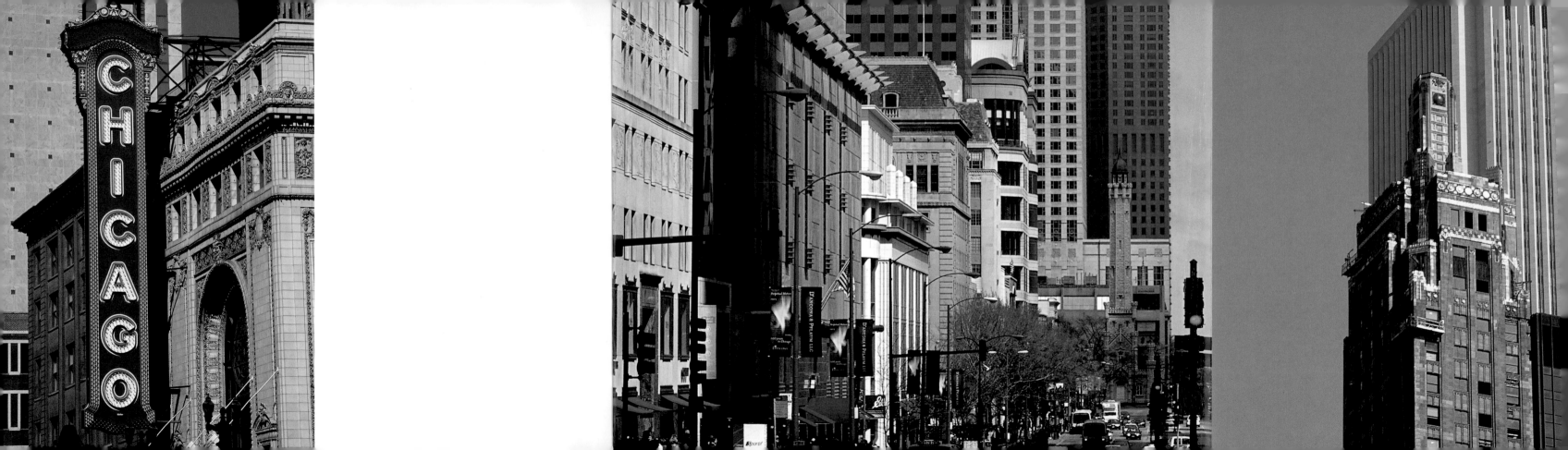

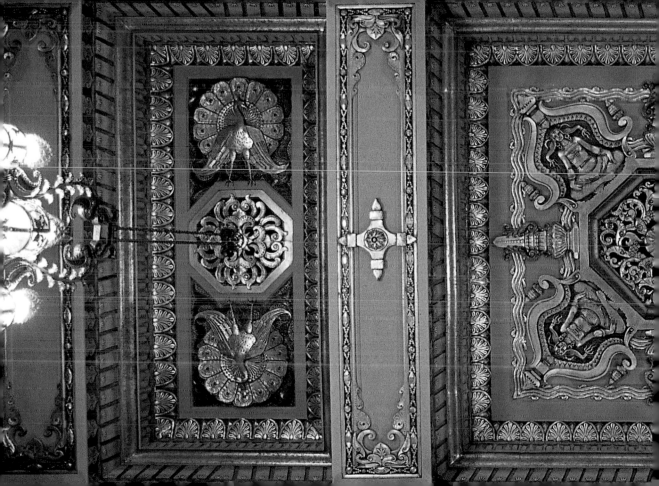

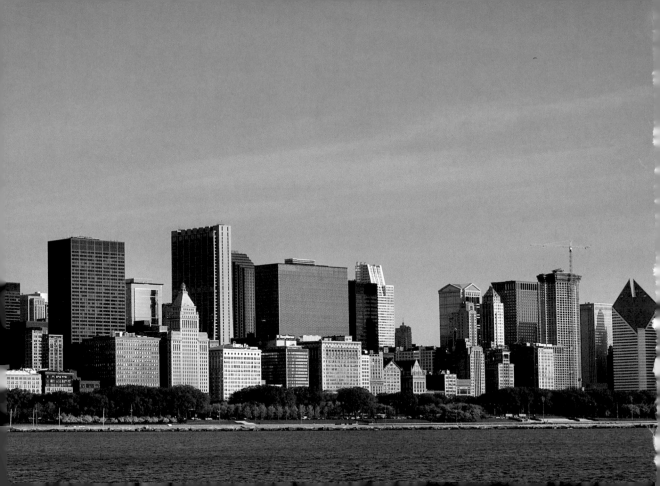

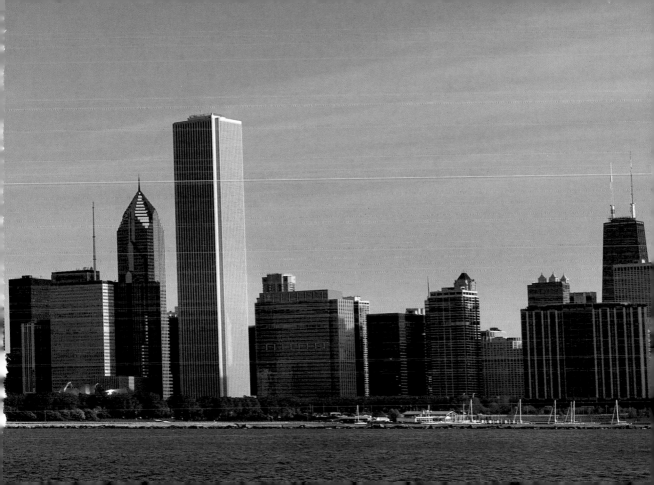

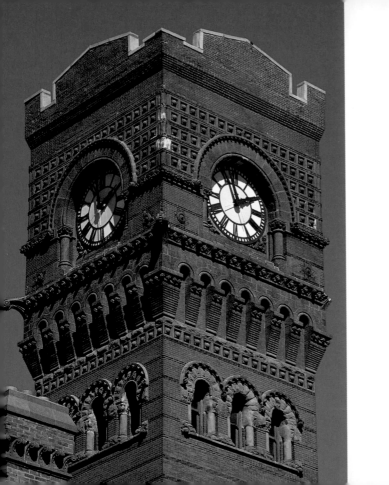

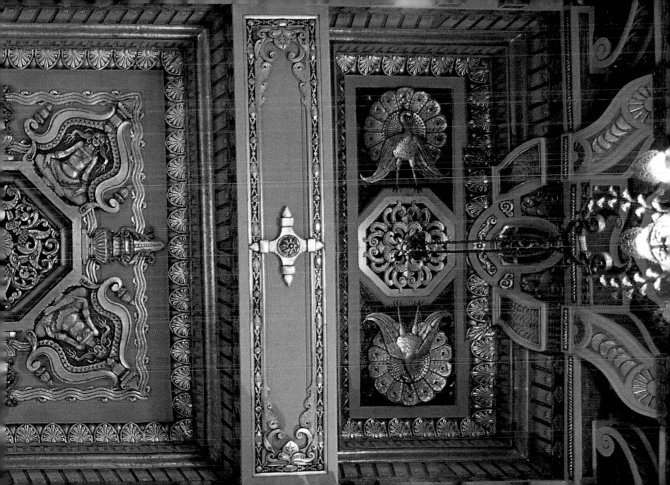

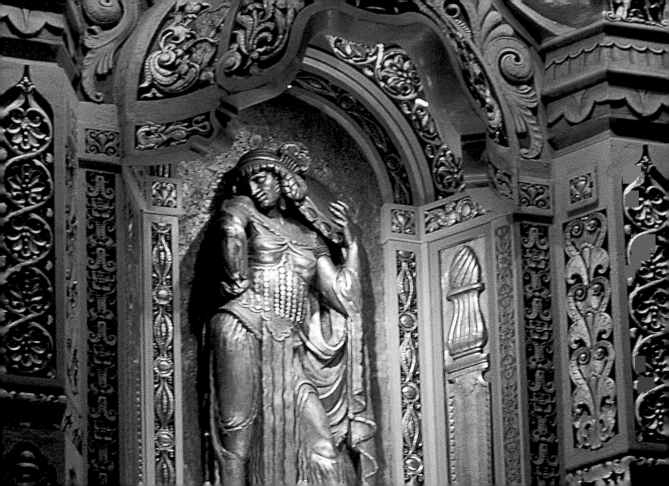

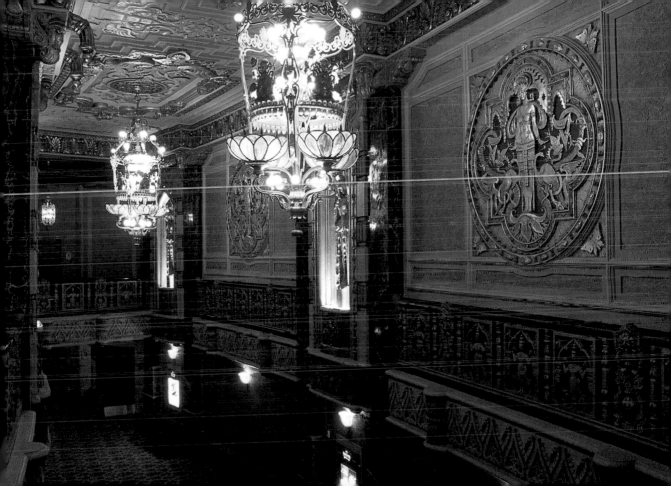

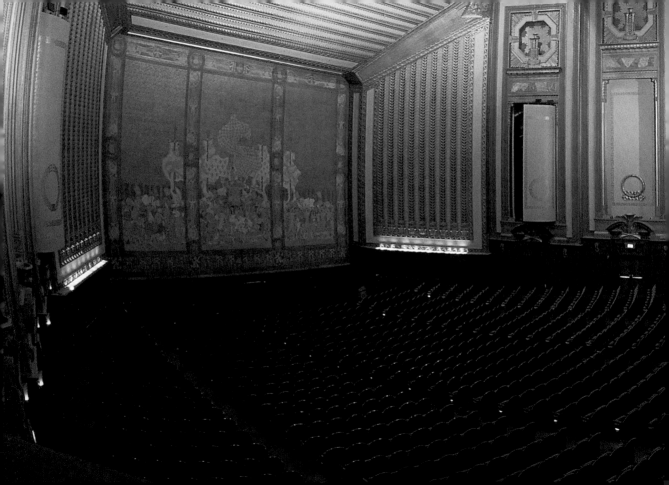

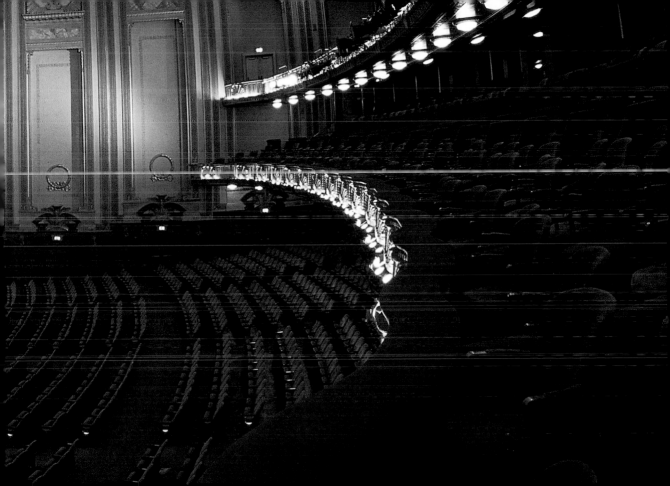

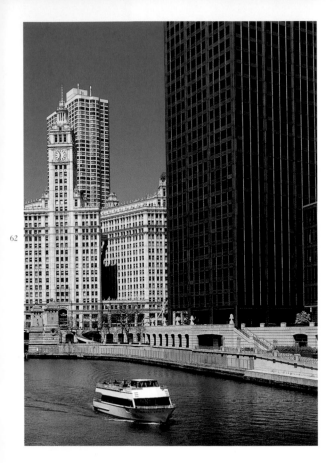

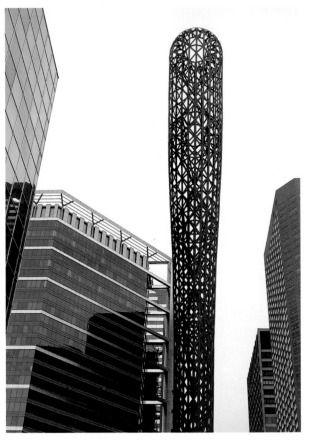

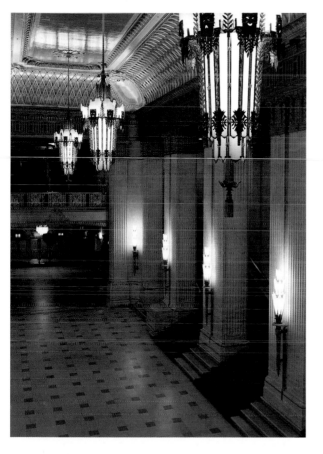

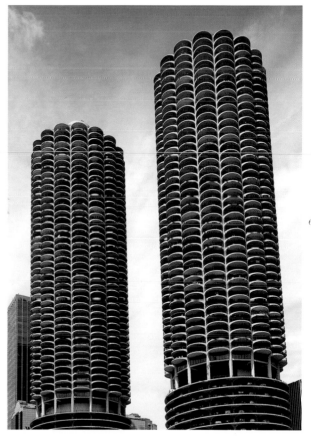

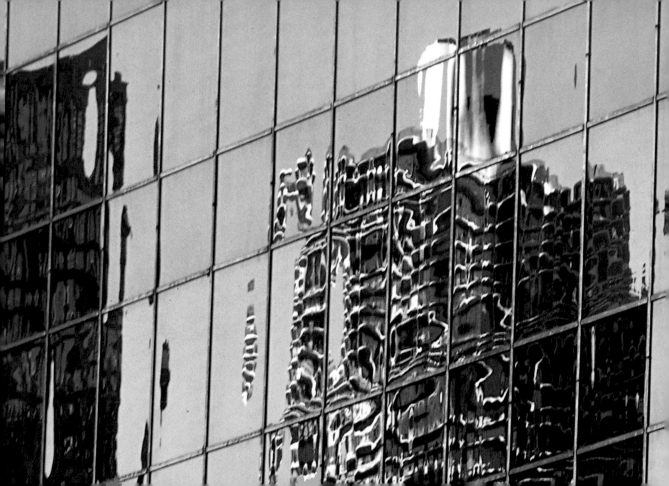

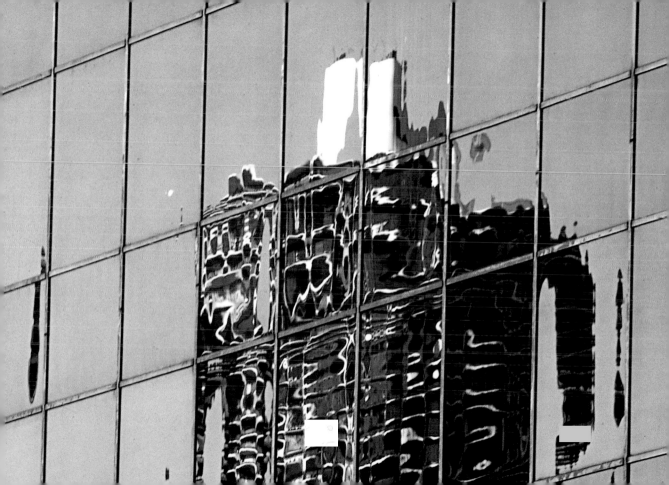

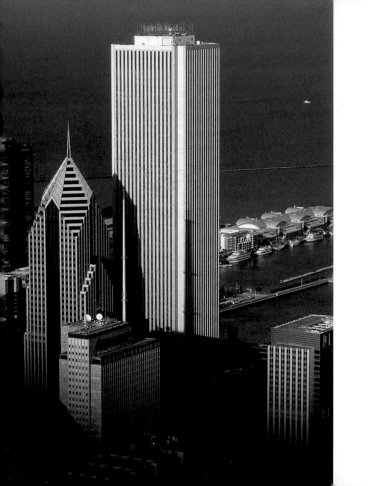

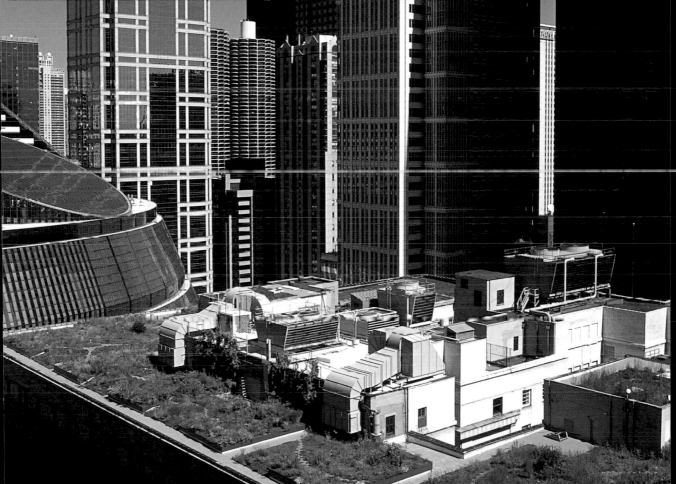

68

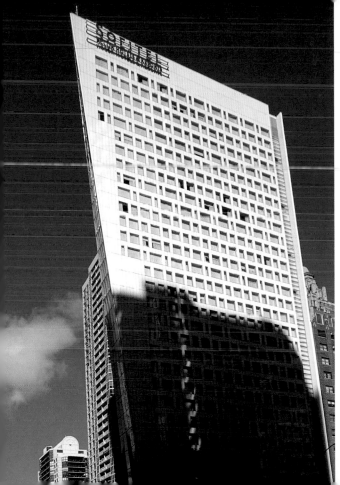

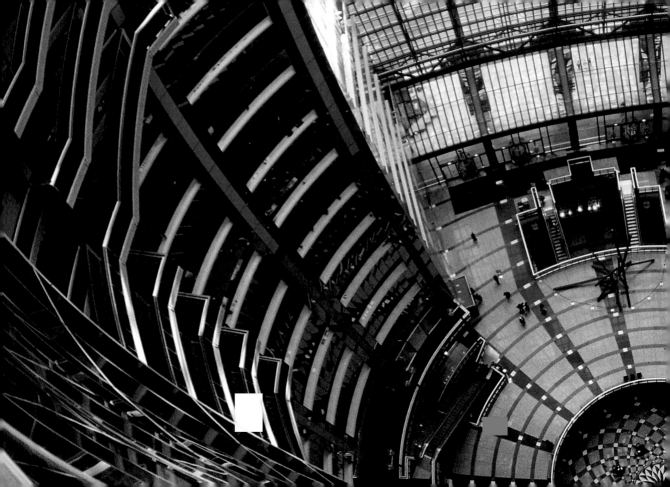

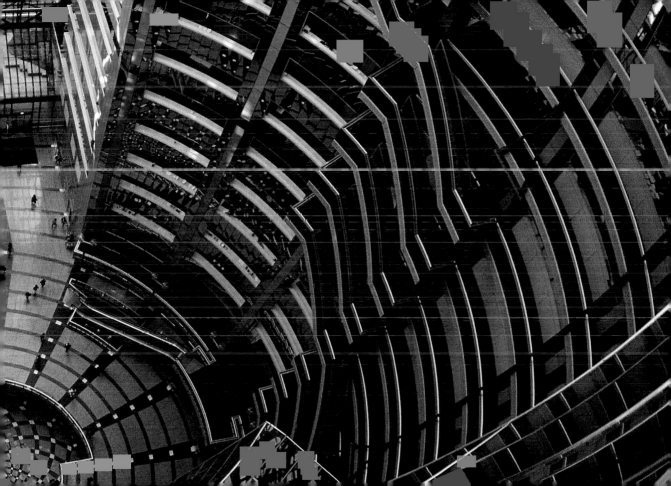

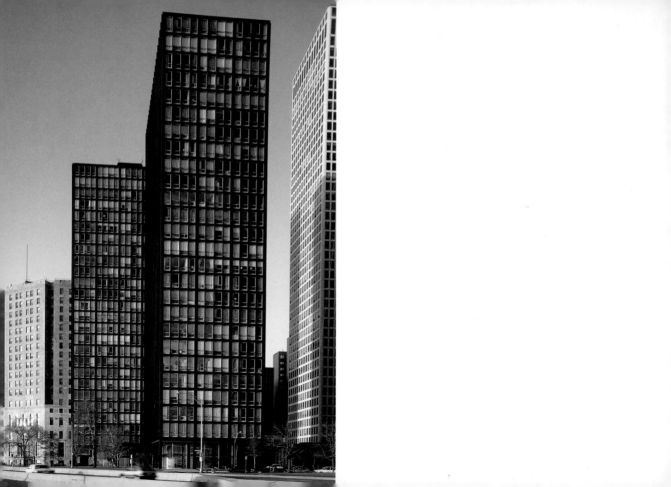

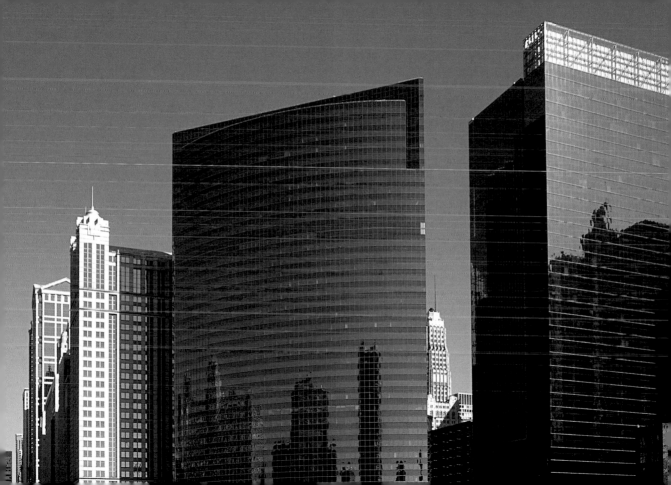

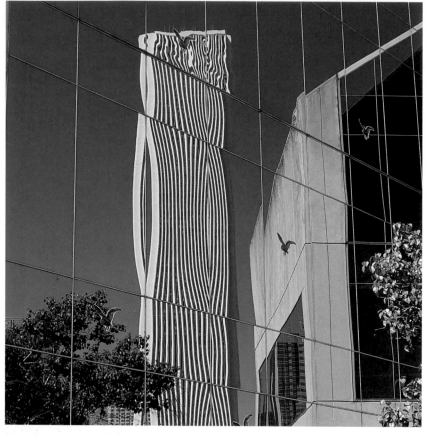

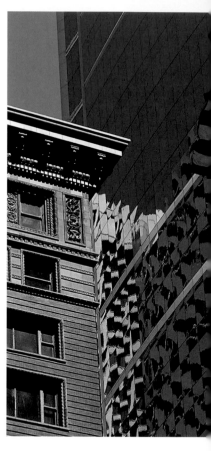

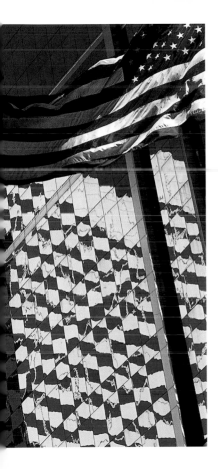

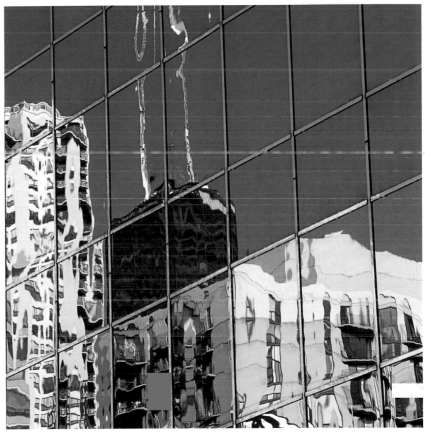

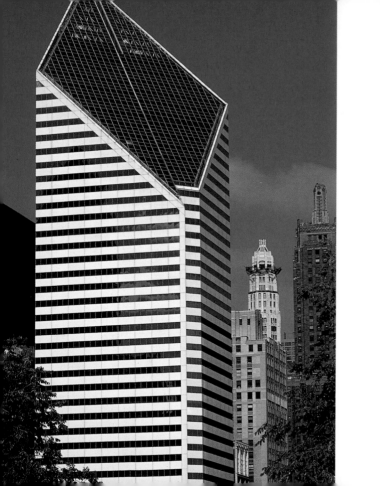

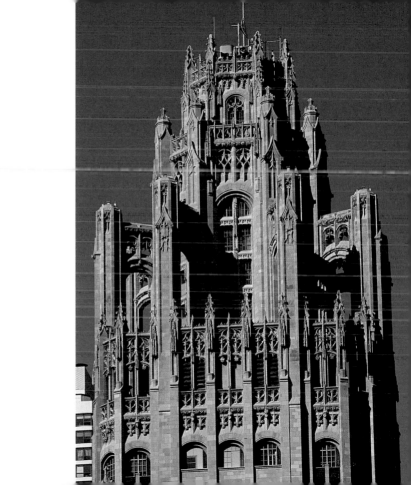

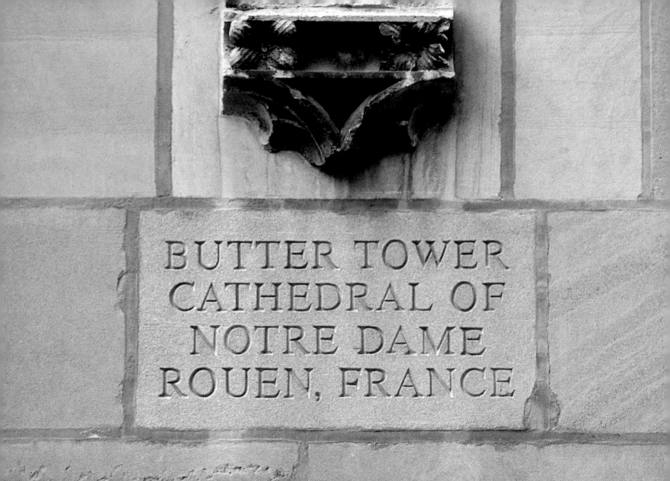

BUTTER TOWER
CATHEDRAL OF
NOTRE DAME
ROUEN, FRANCE

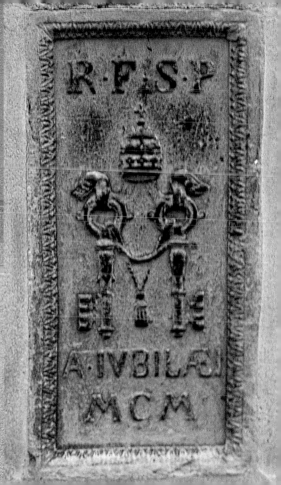

REIMS CATHEDRAL
REIMS FRANCE

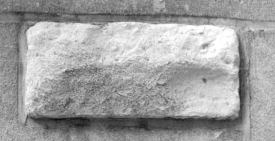

UNION STOCK YARDS GATE
CHICAGO

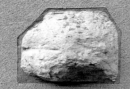

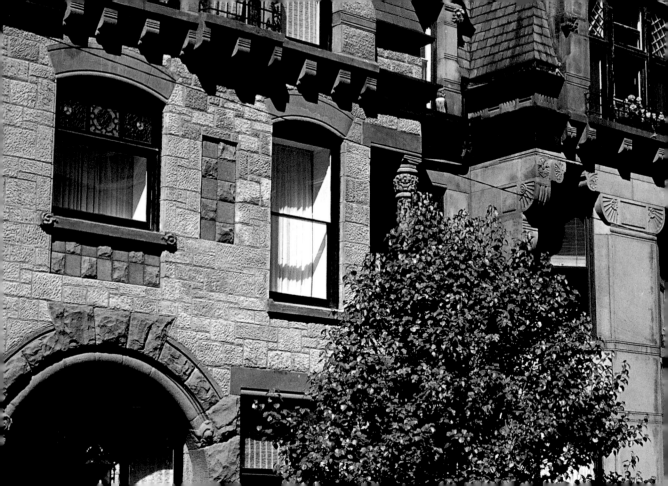

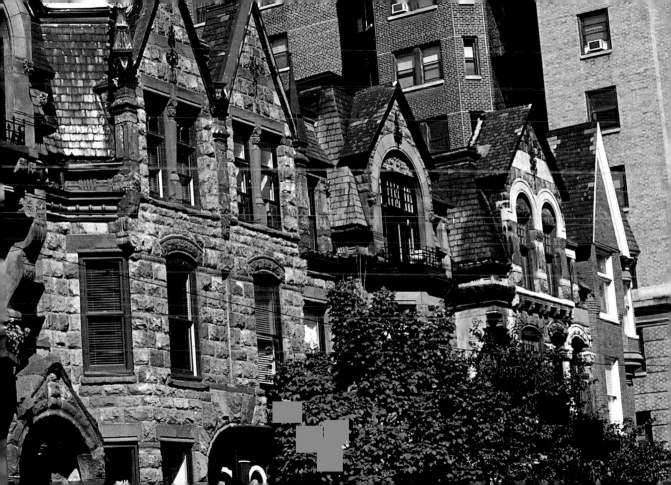

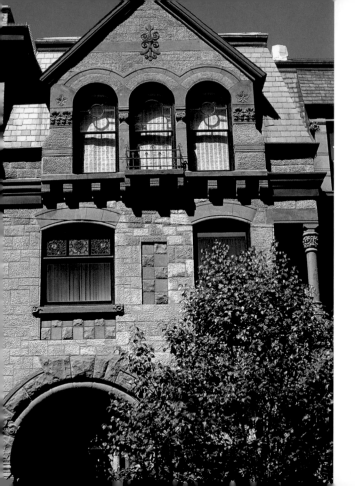

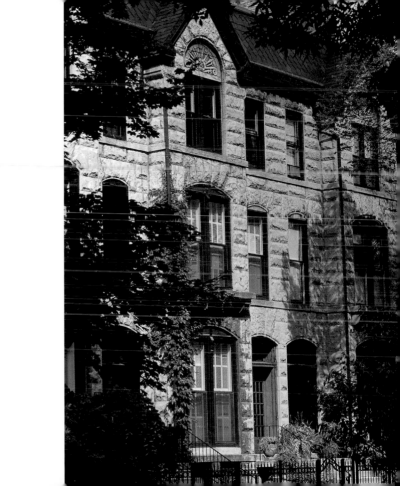

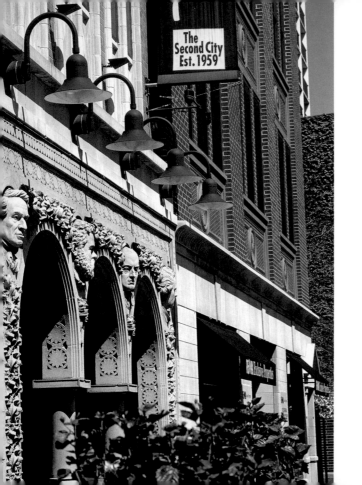

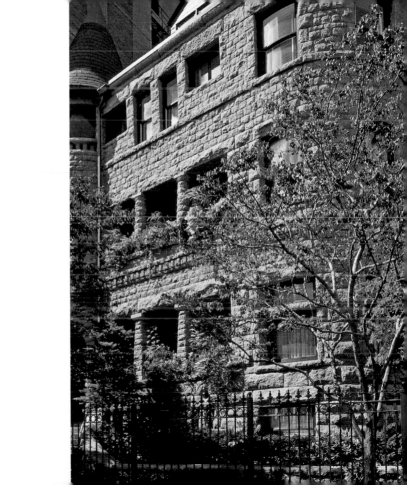

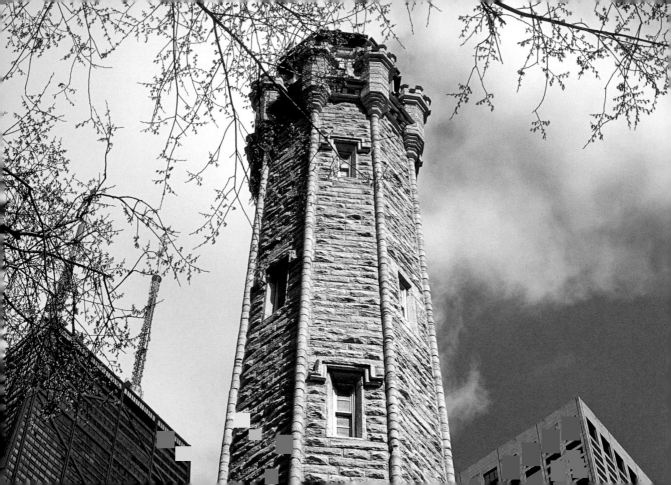

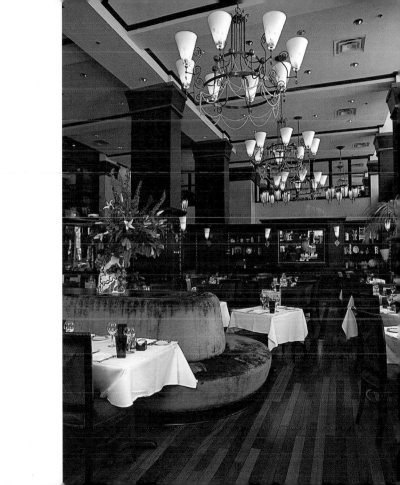

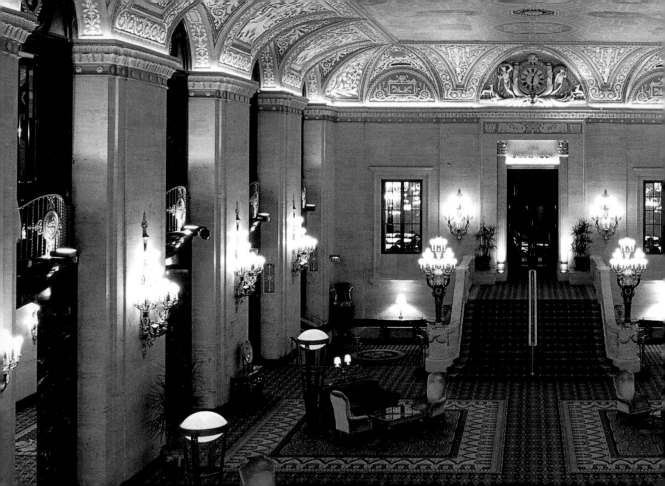

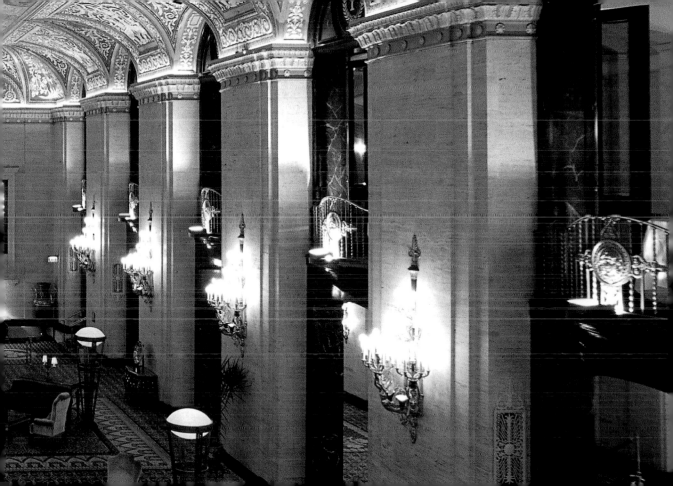

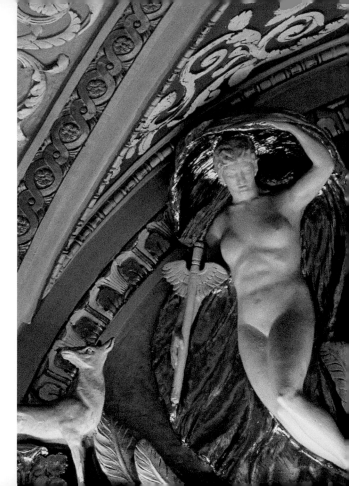

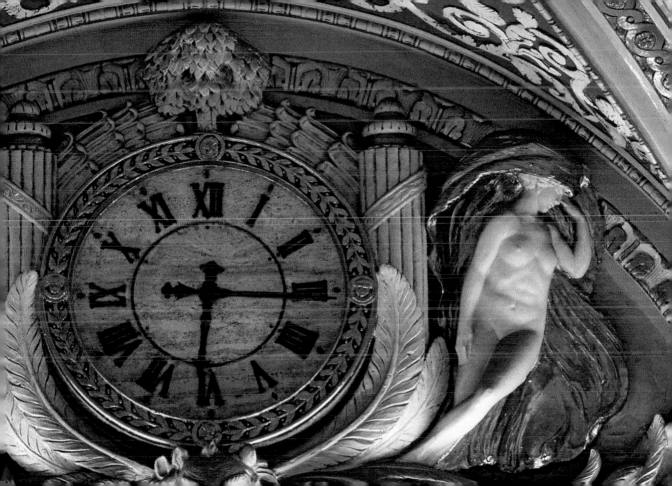

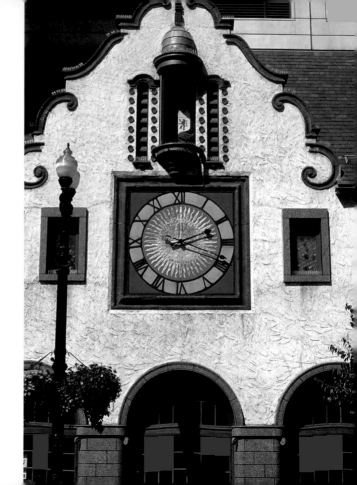

92

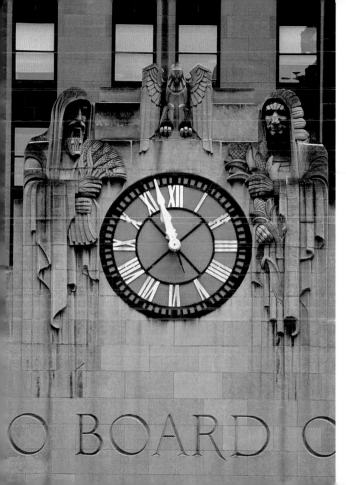

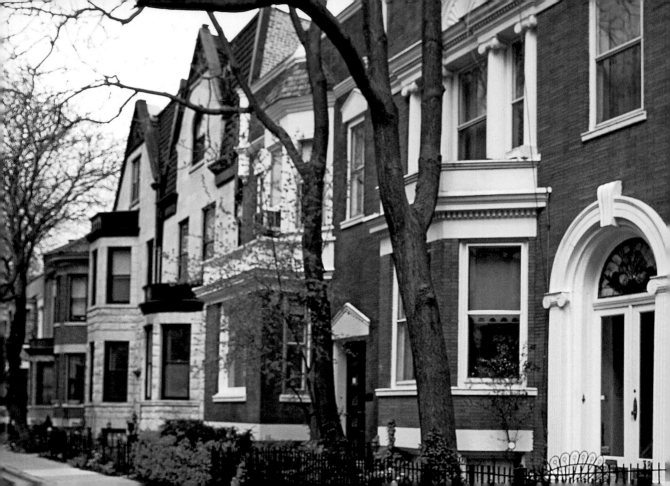

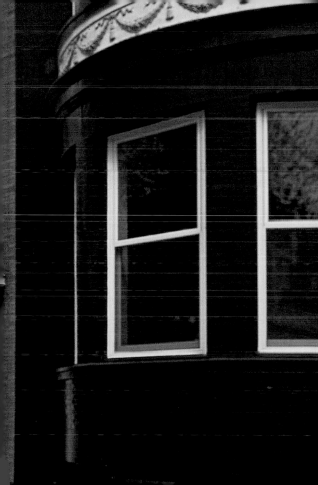

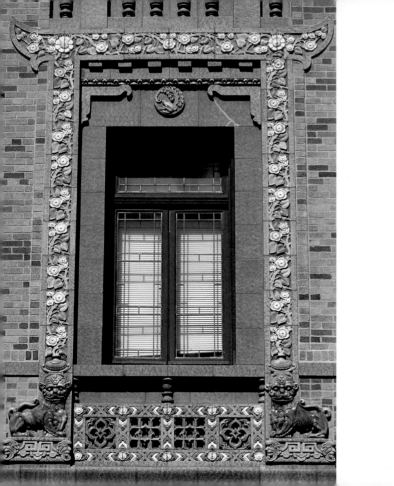

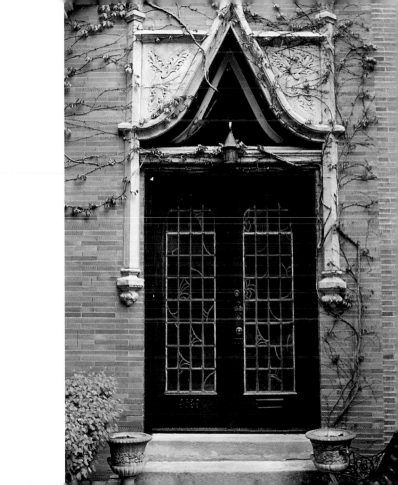

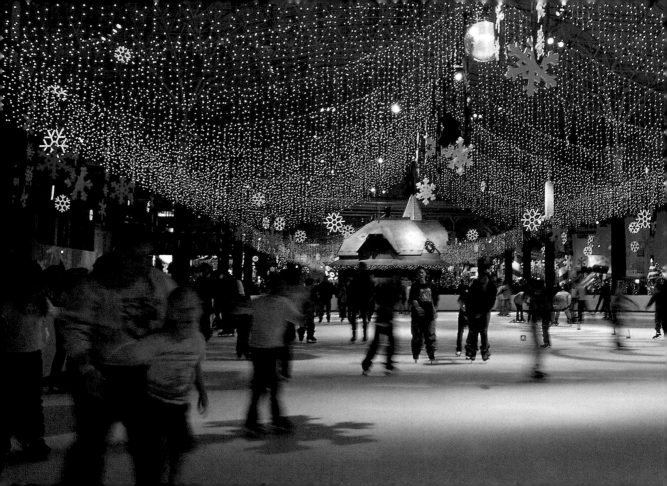

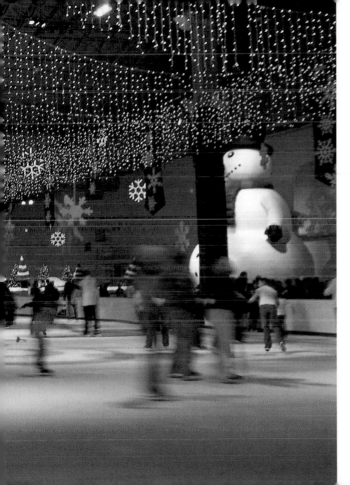

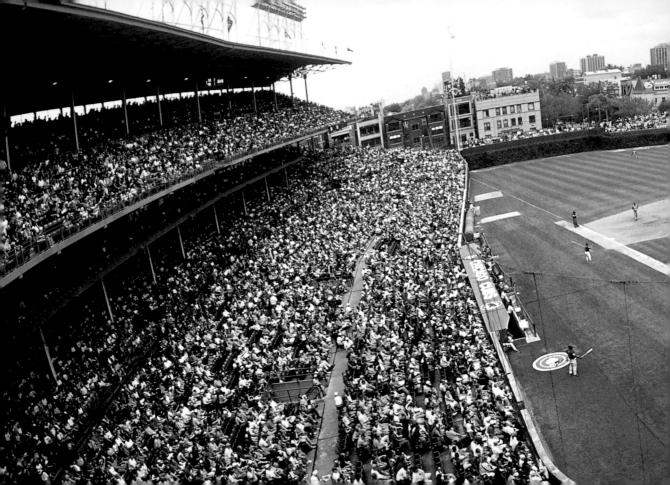

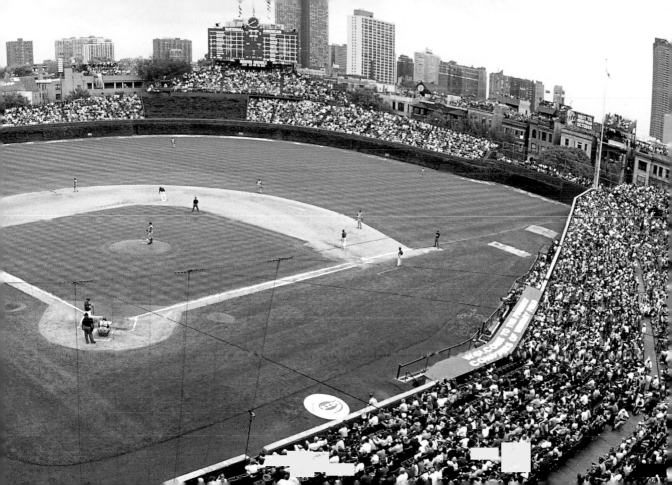

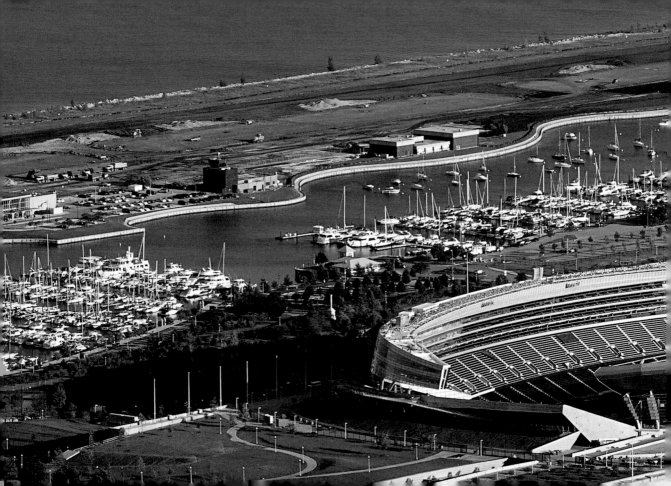

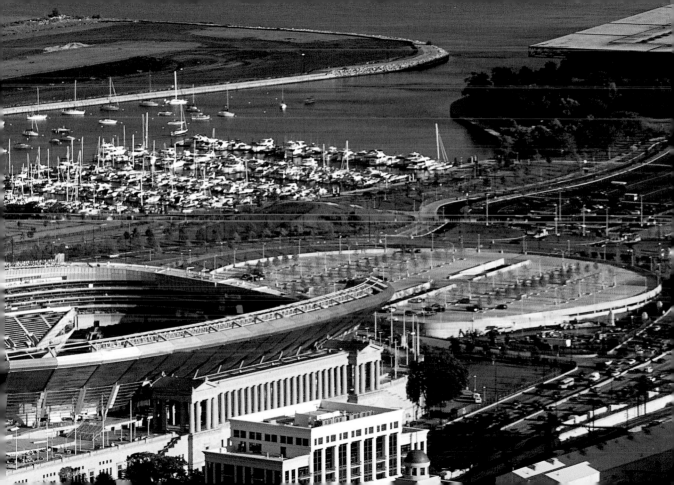

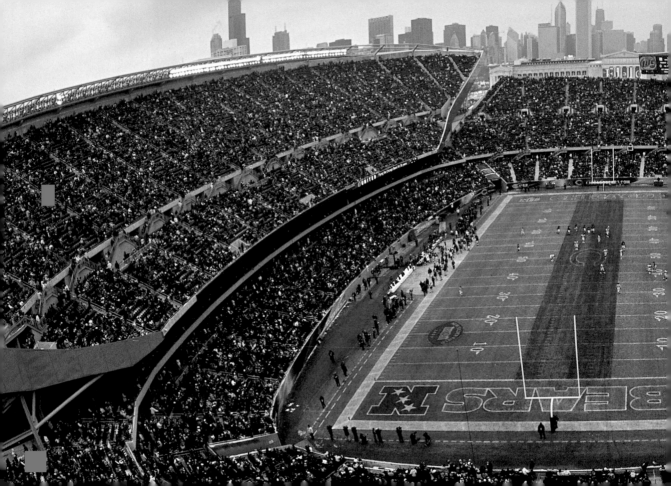

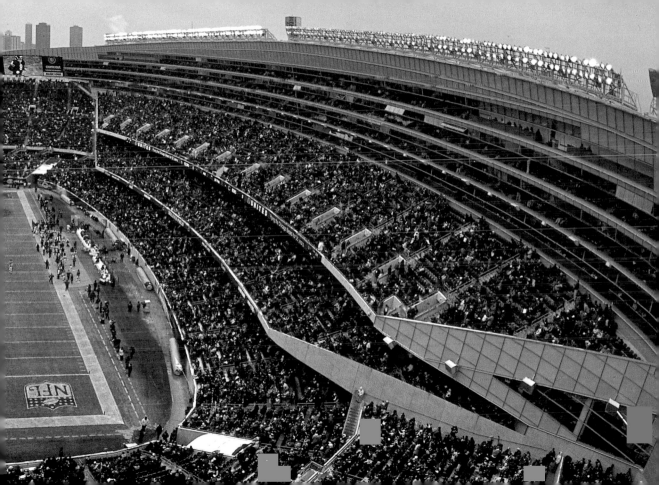

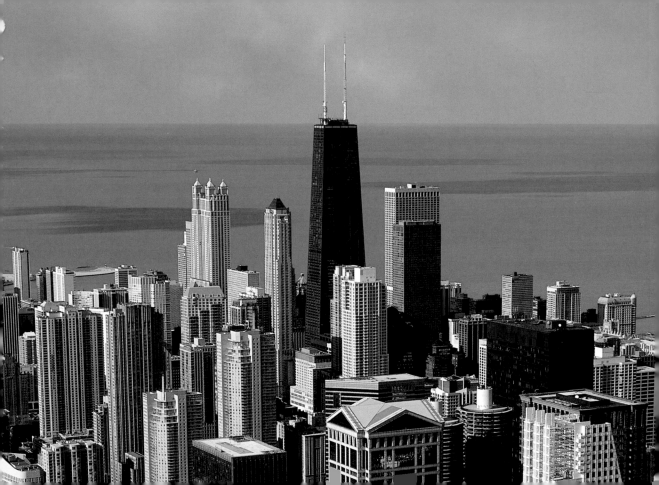

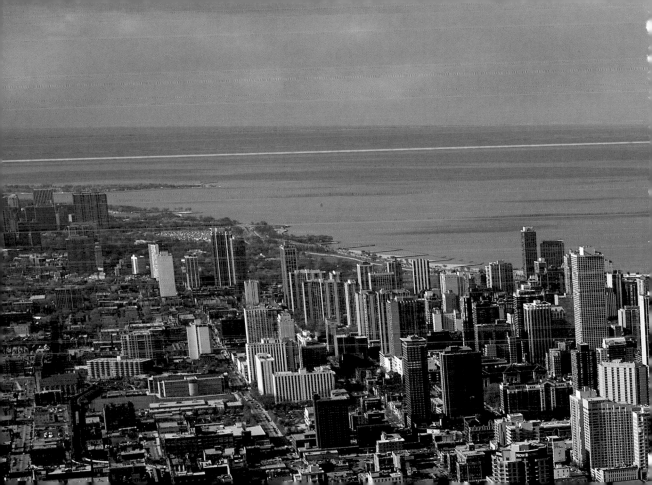

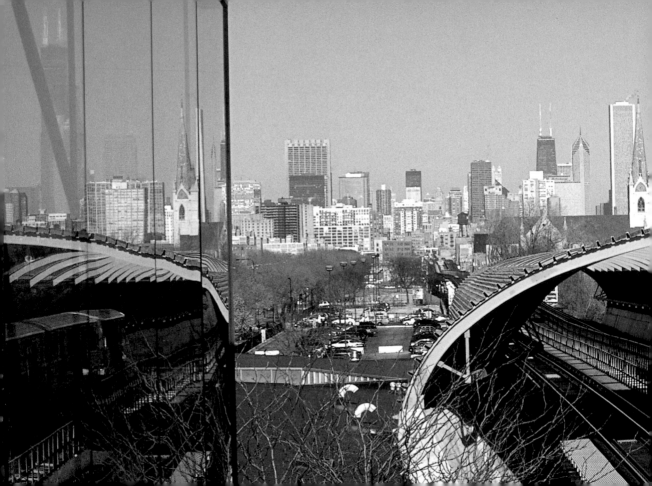

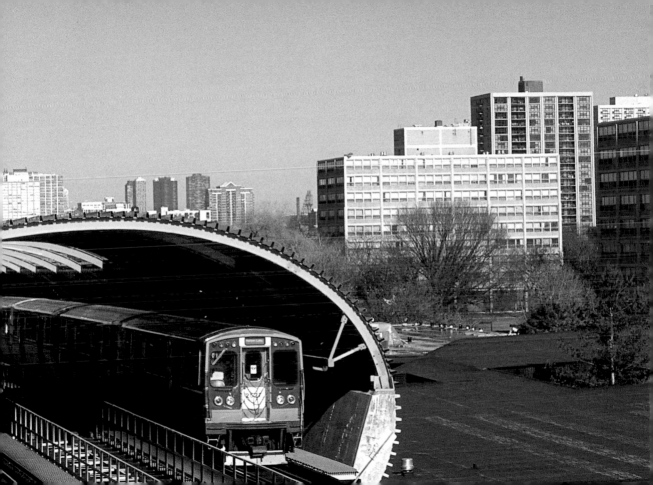

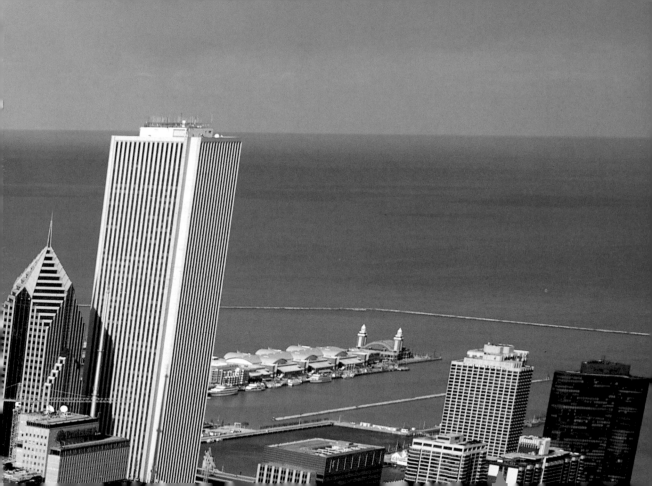

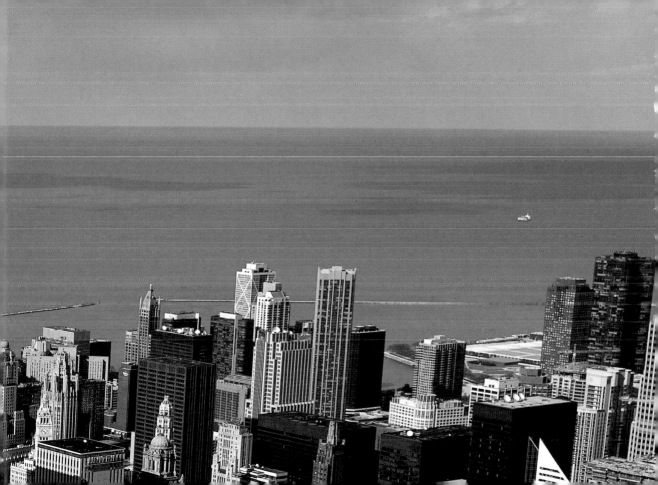

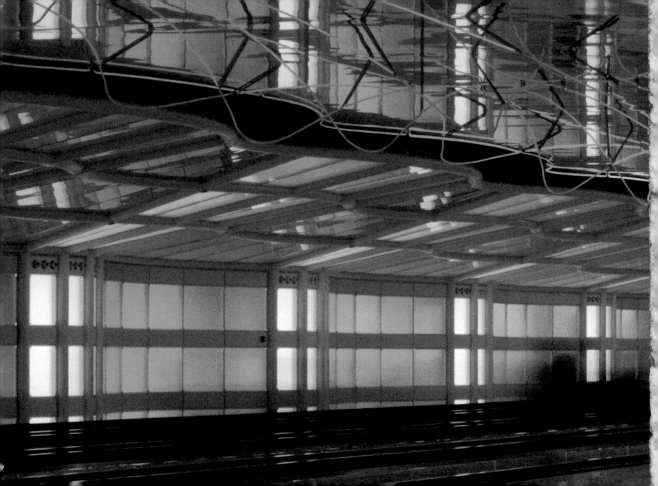

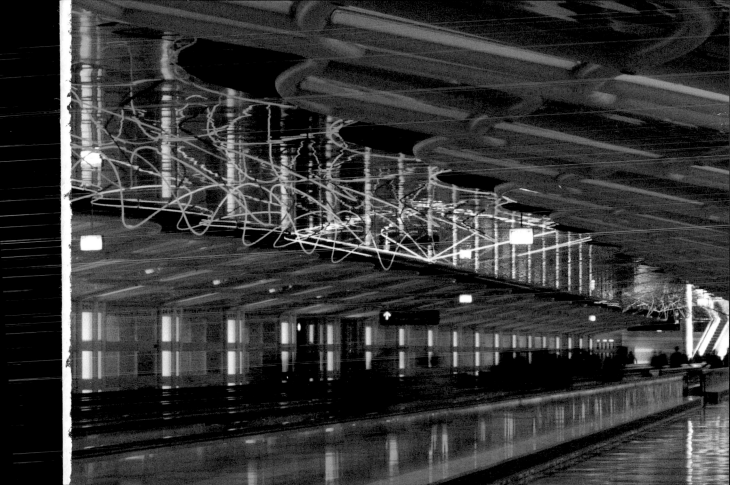

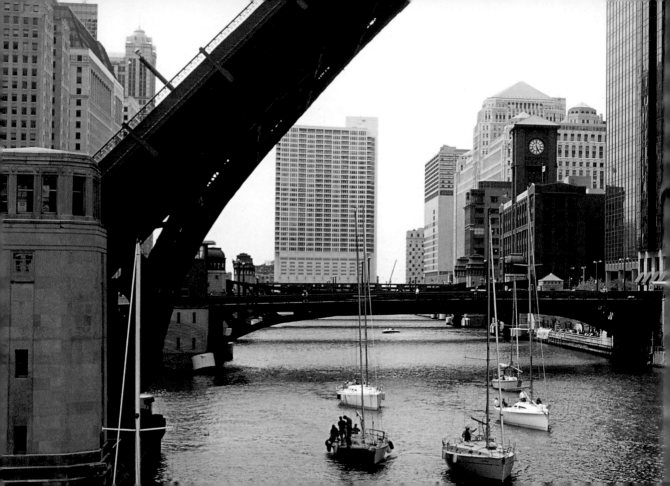

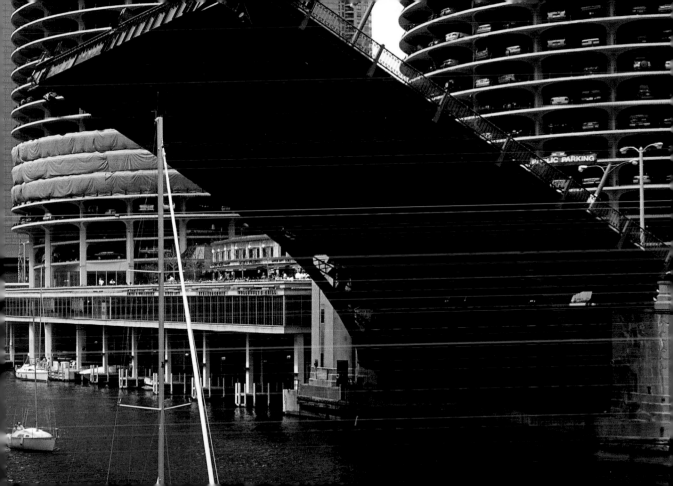

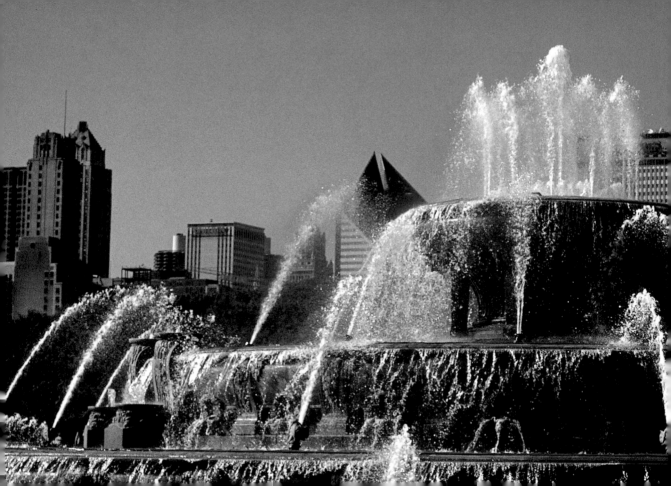

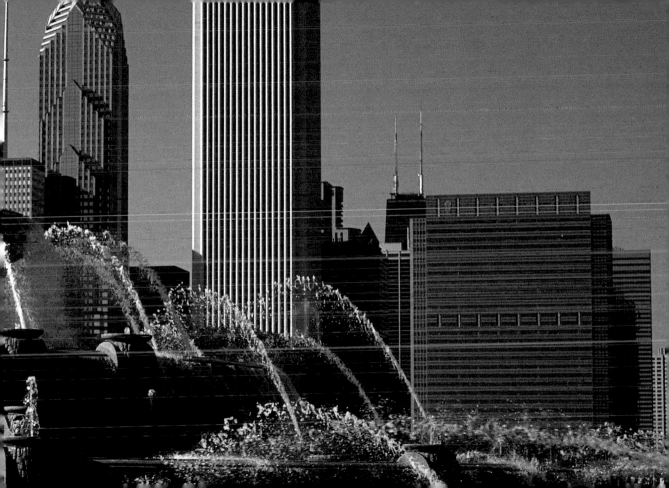

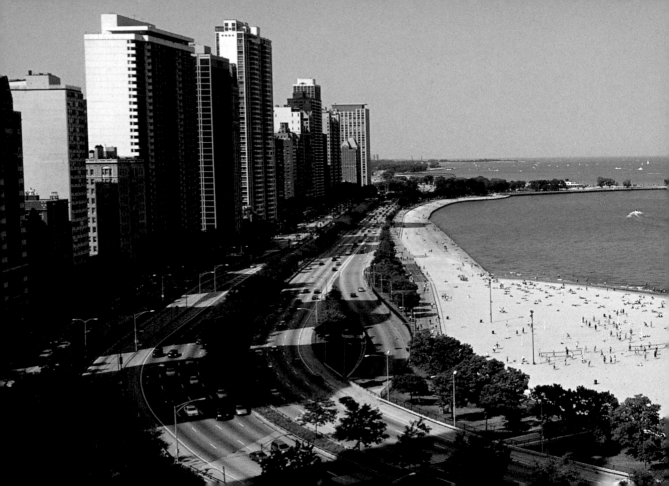

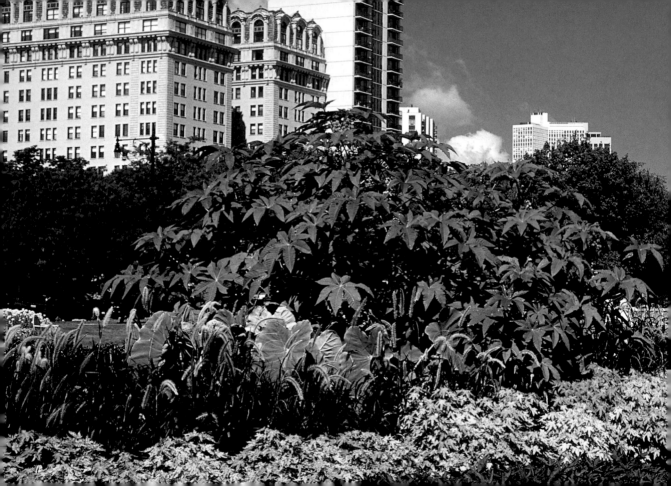

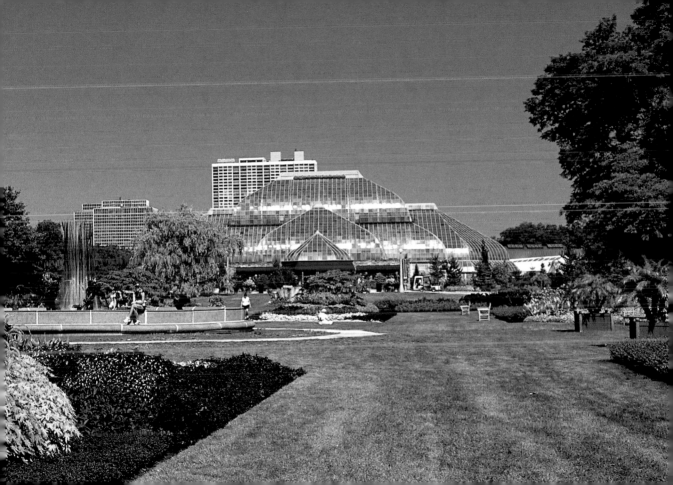

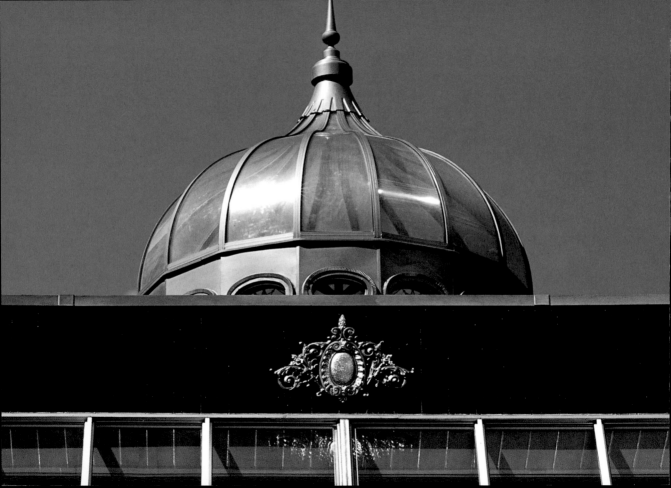

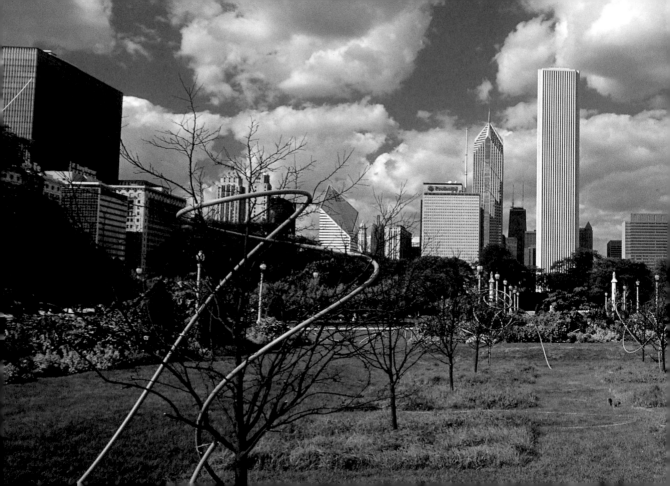

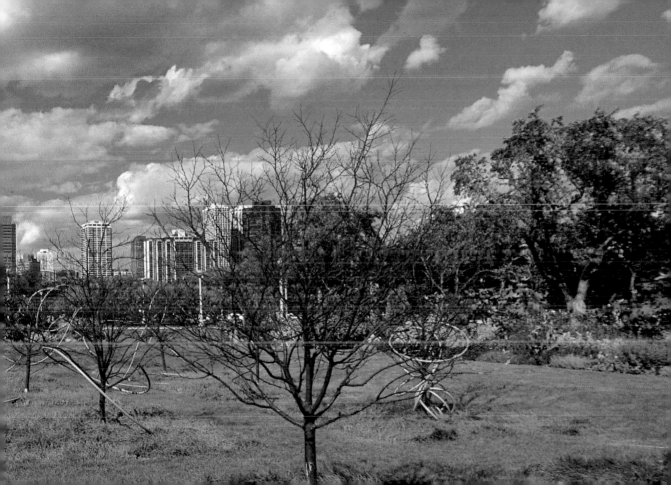

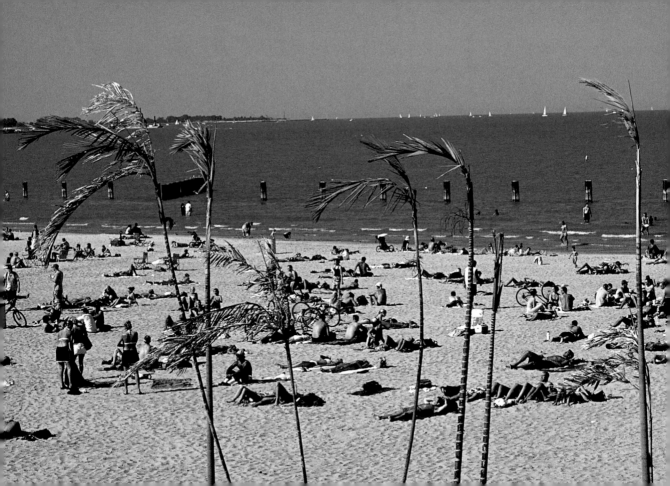

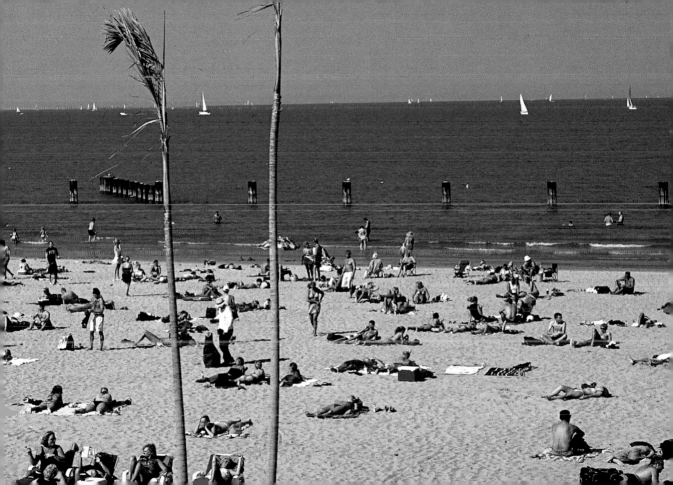

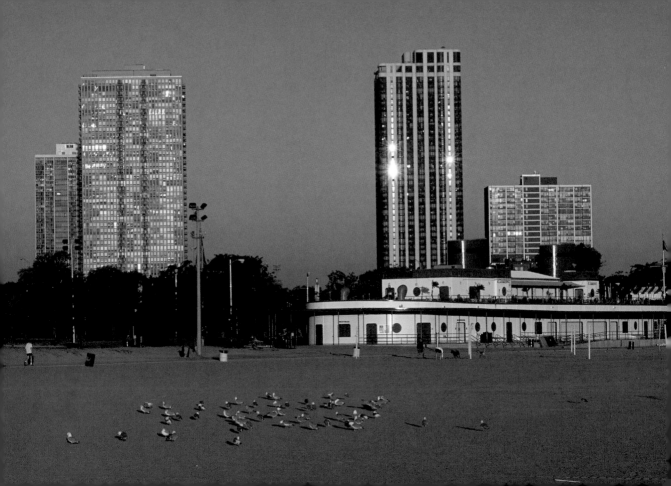

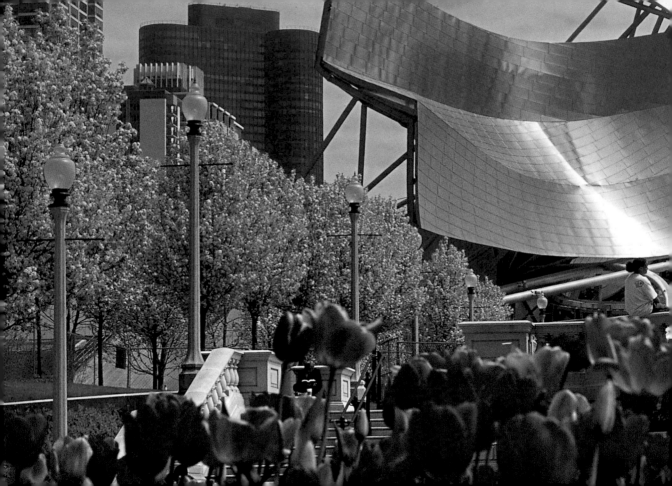

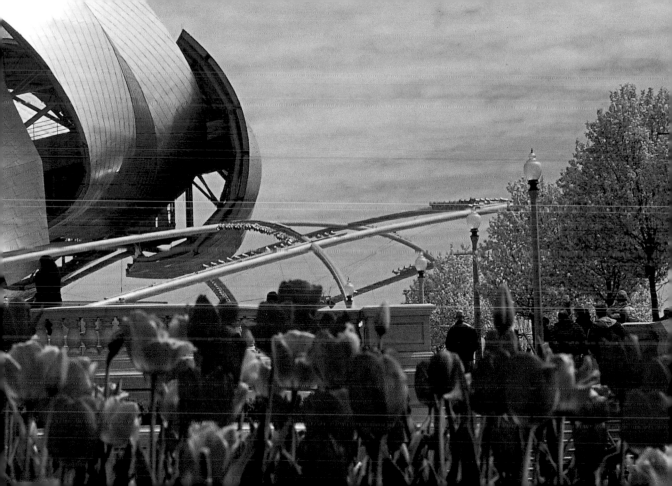

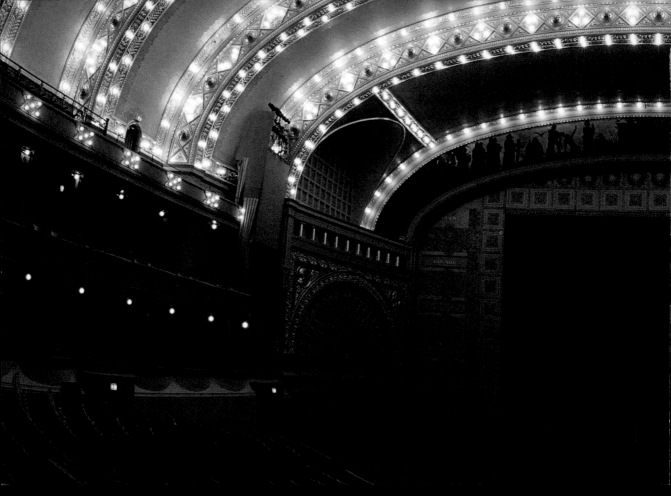

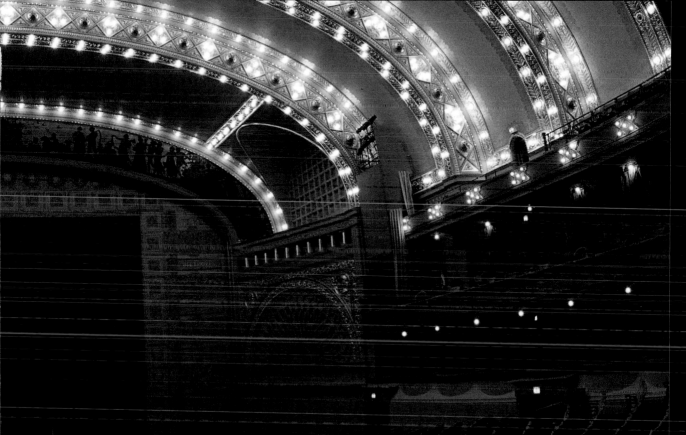

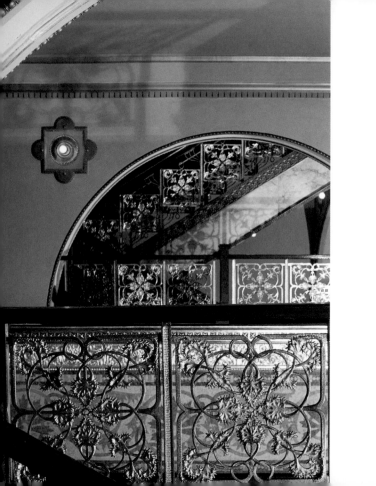

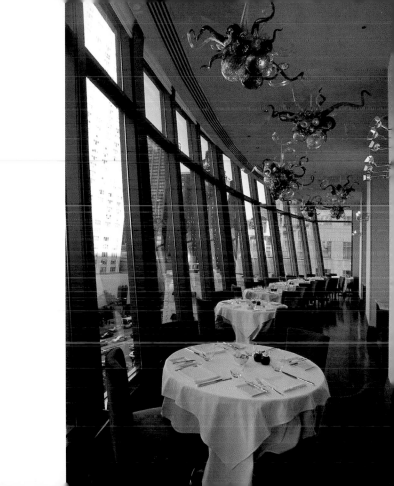

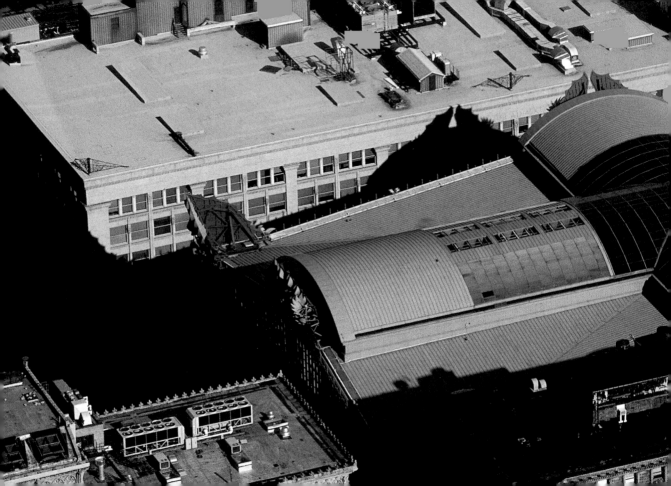

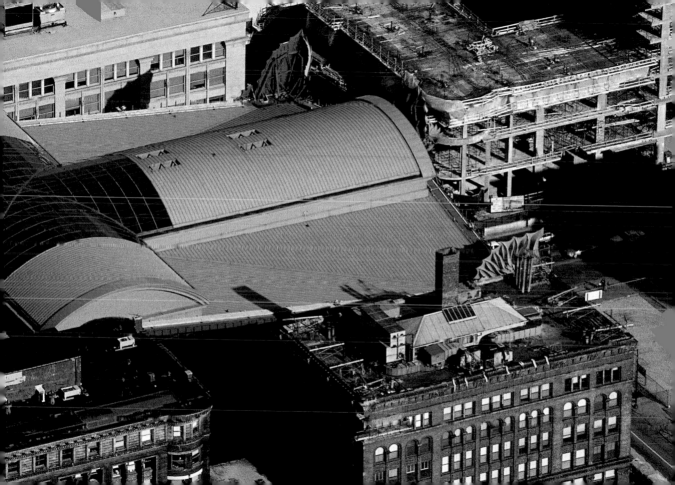

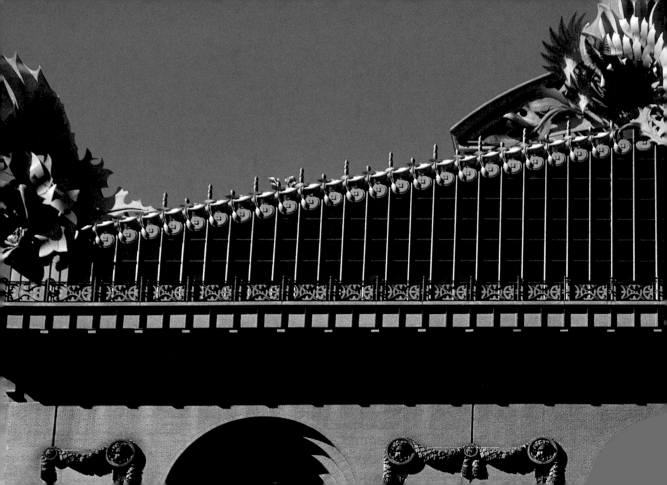

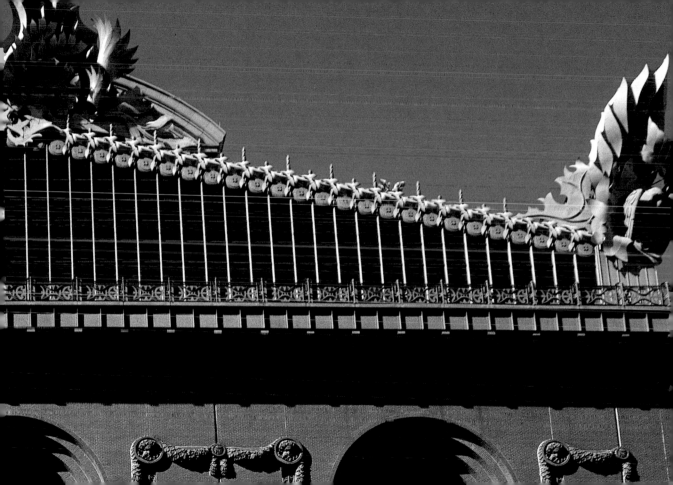

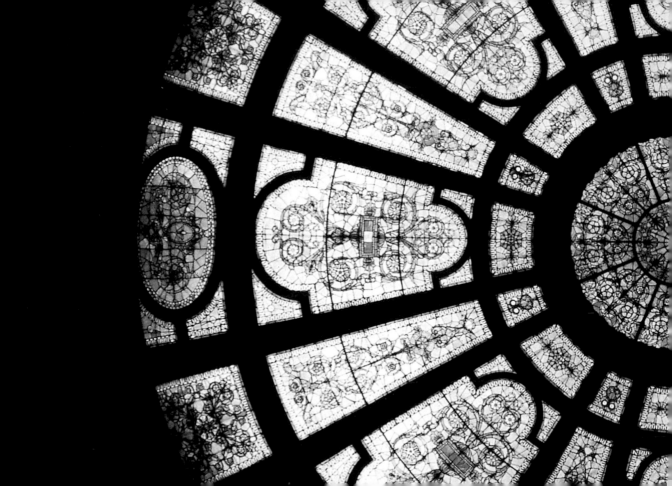

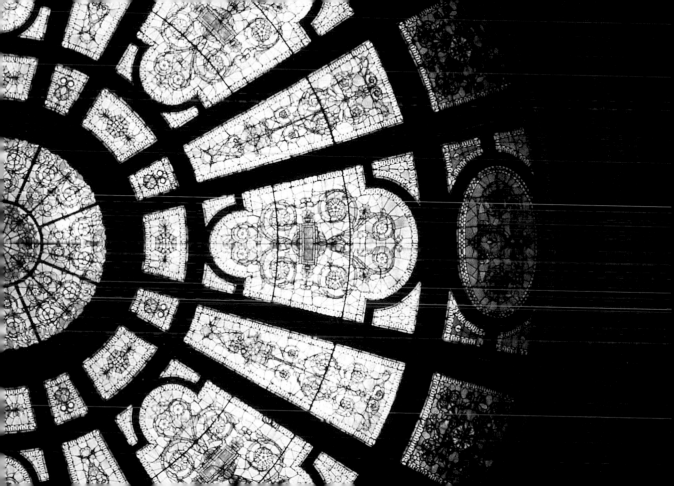

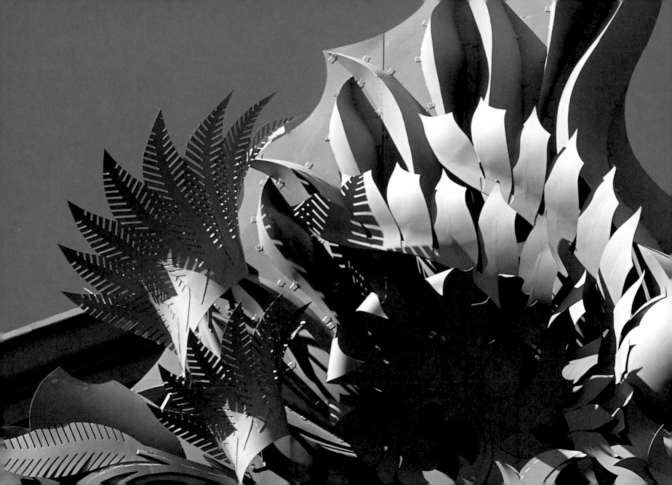

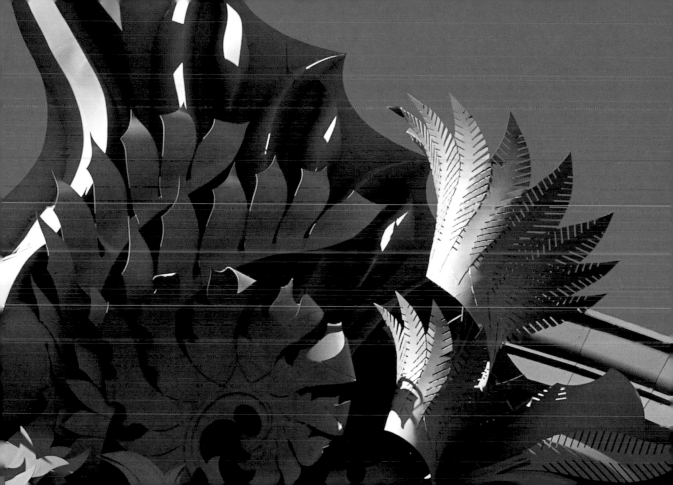

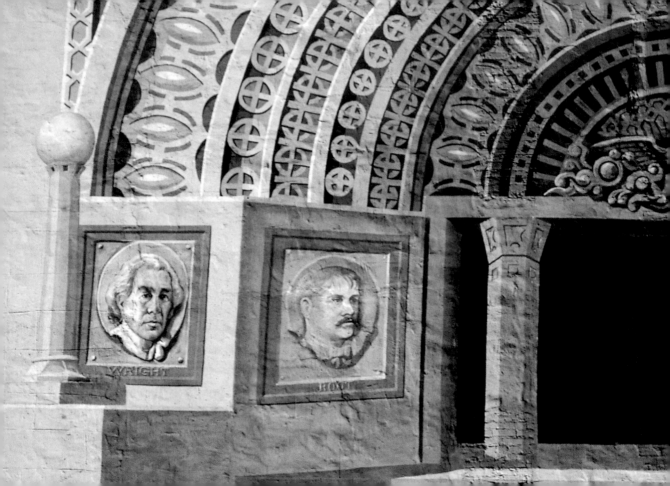

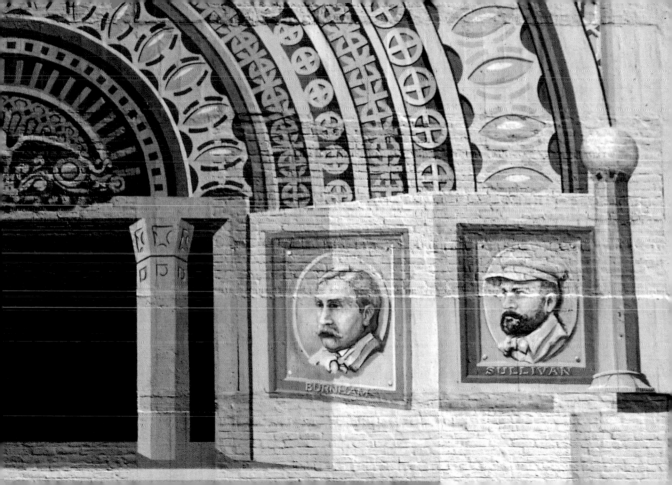

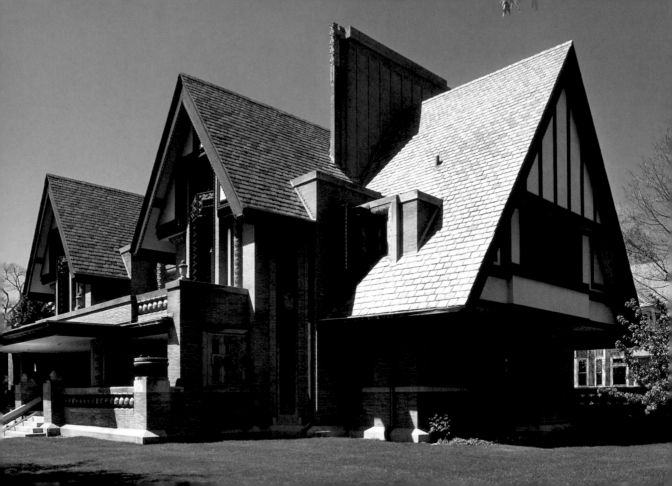

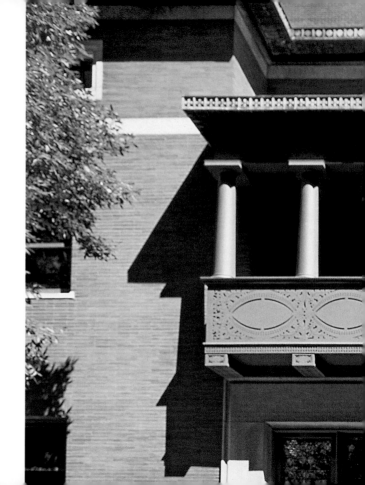

148

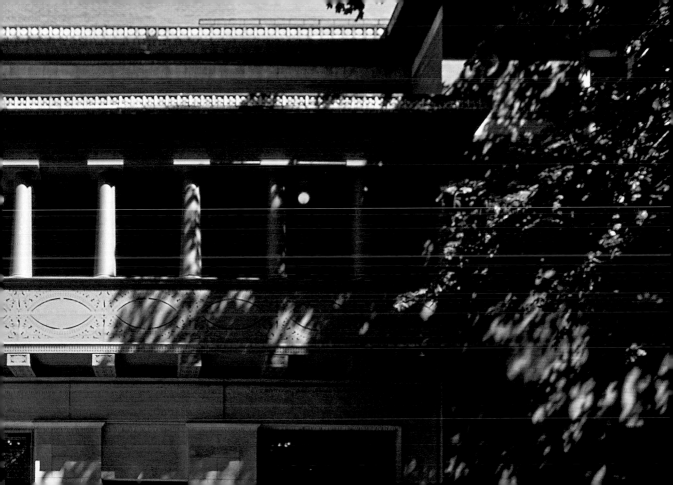

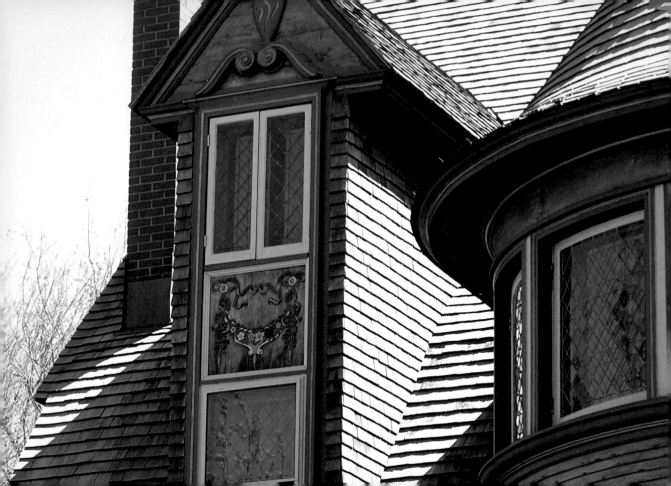

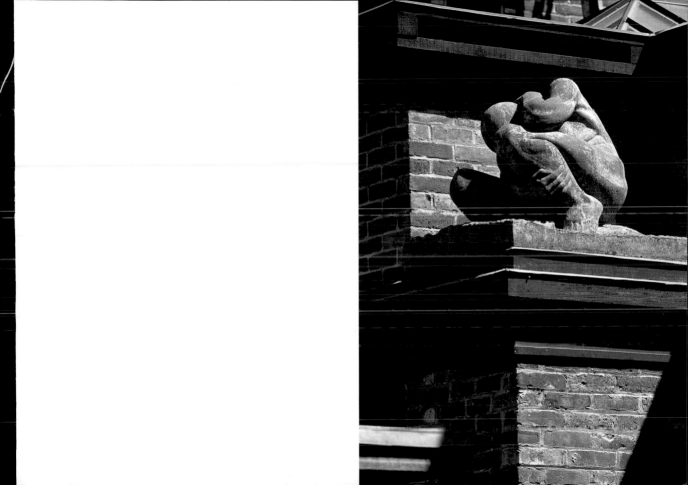

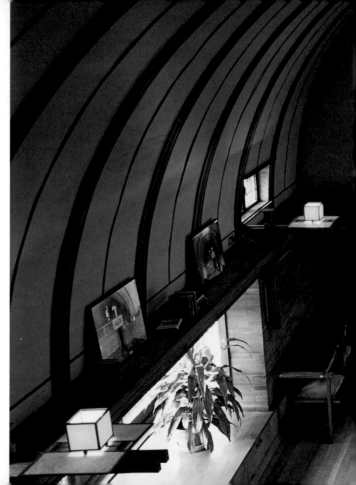

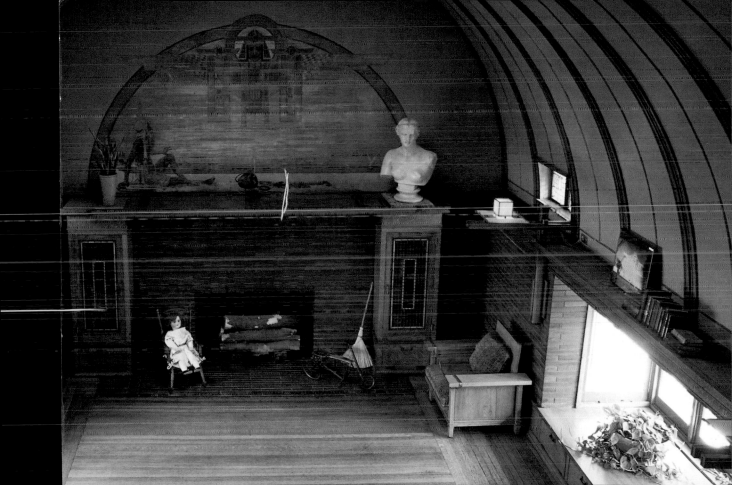

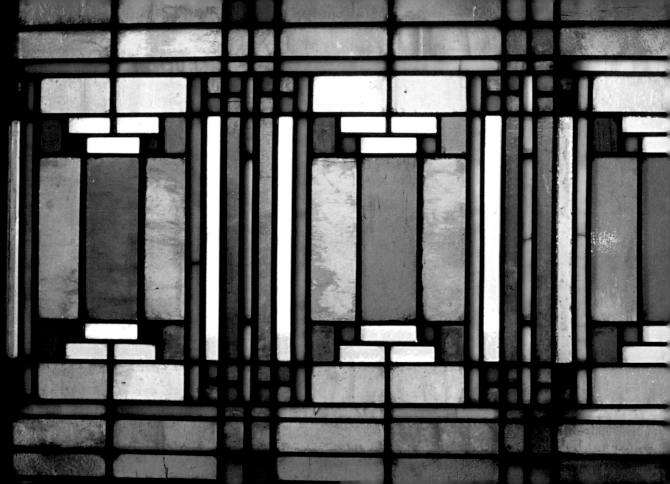

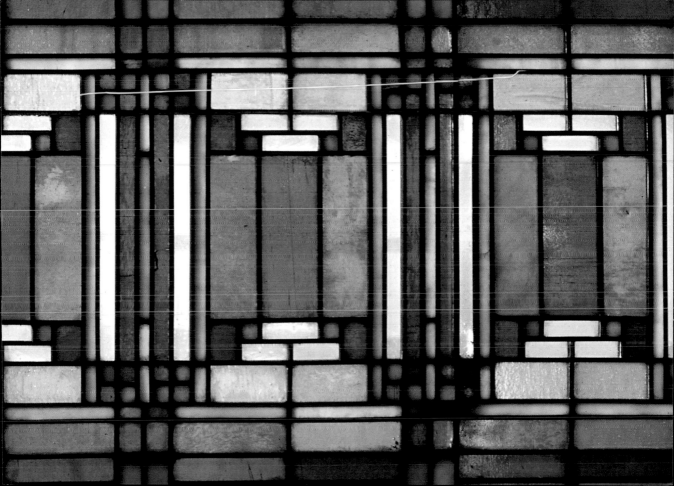

156

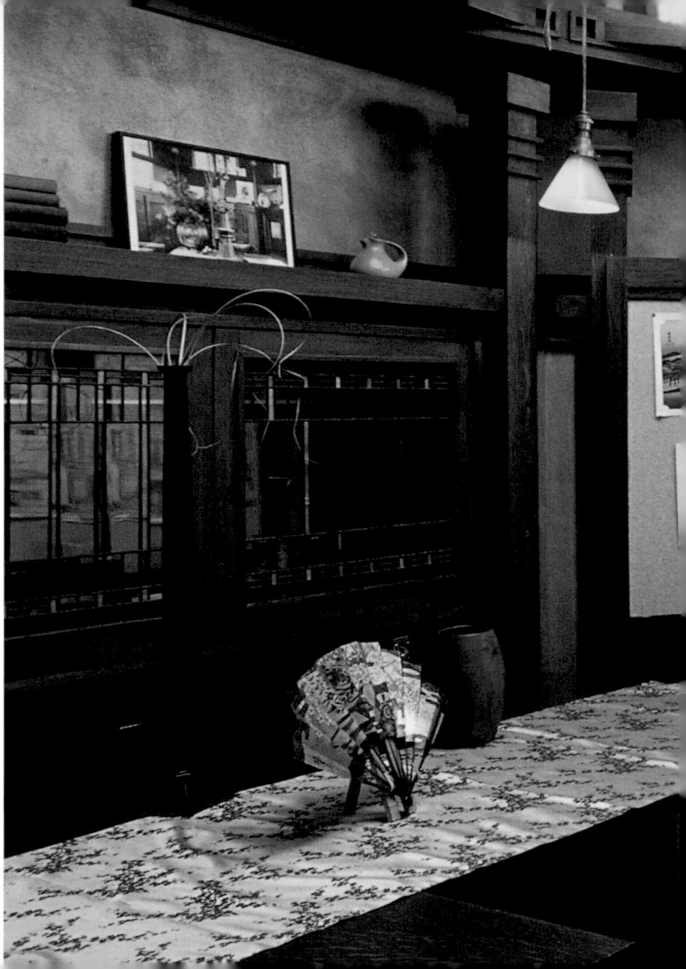

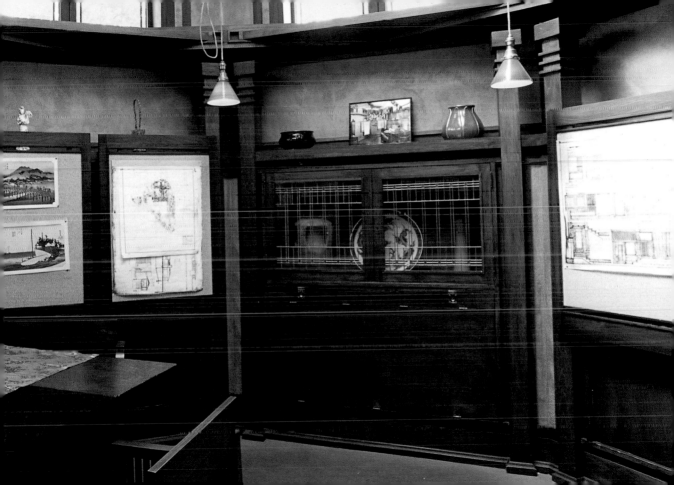

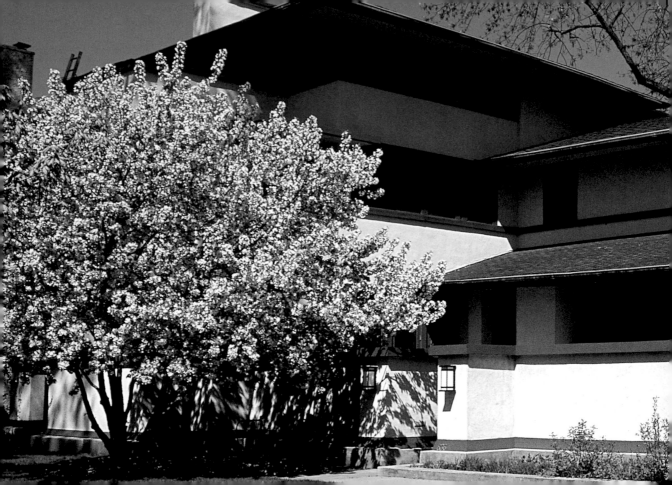

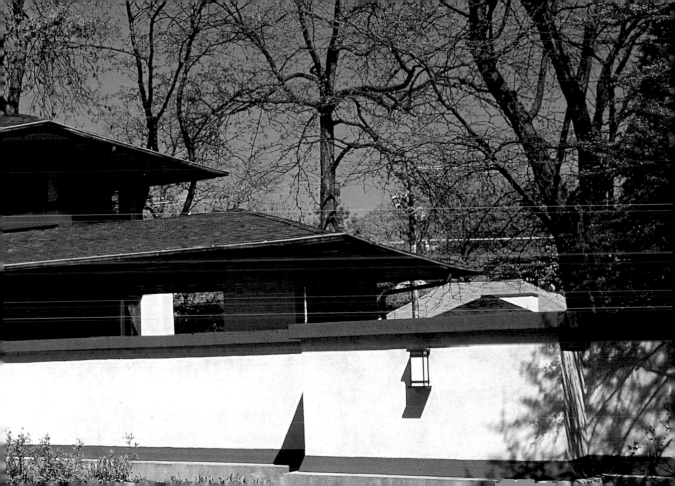

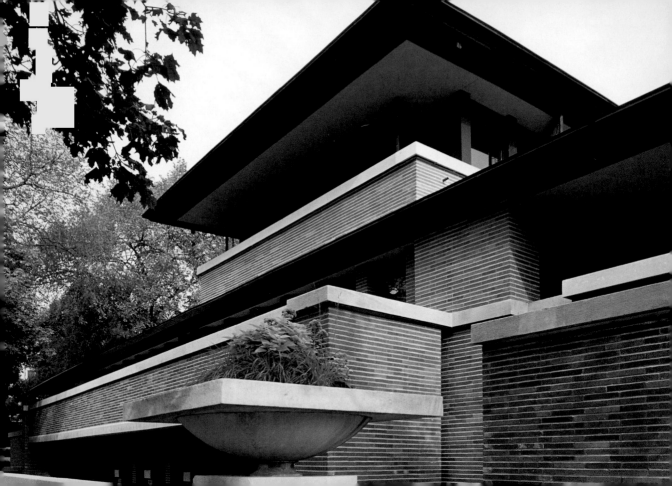

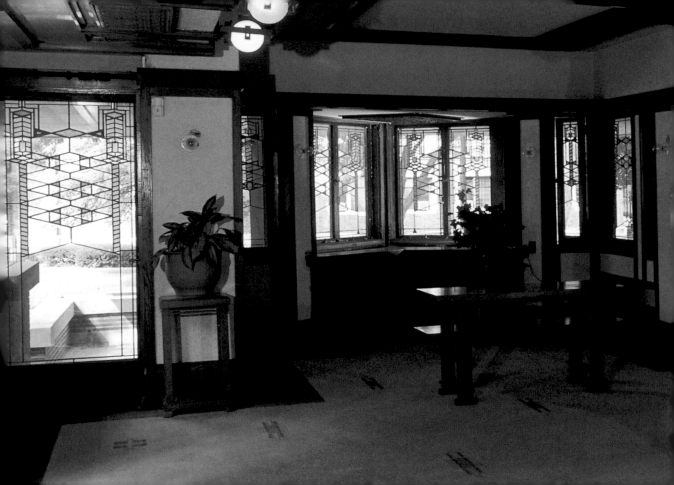

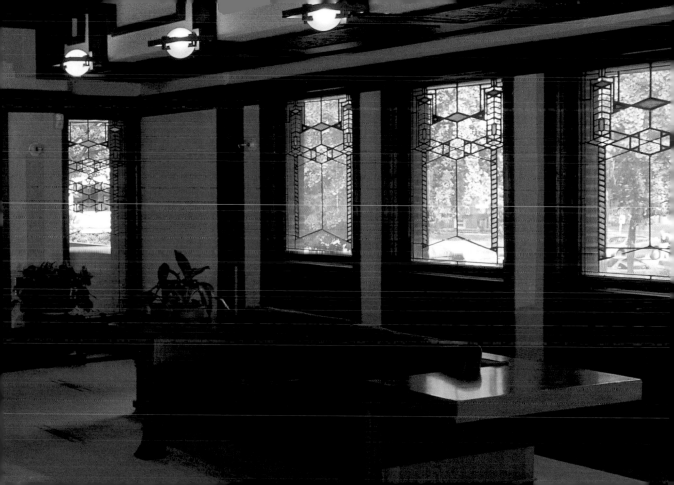

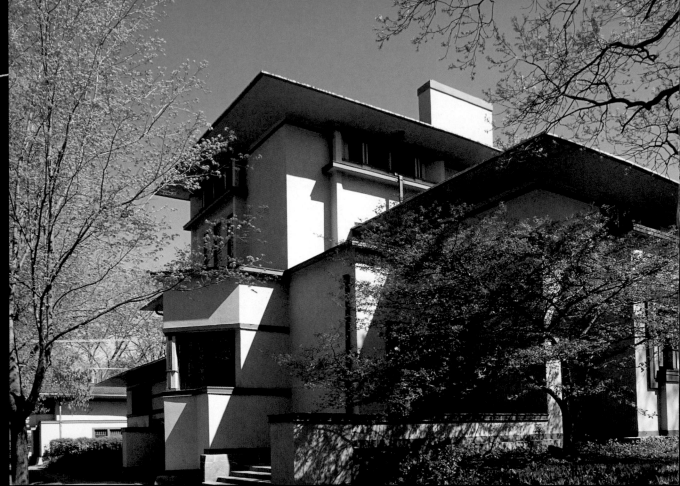

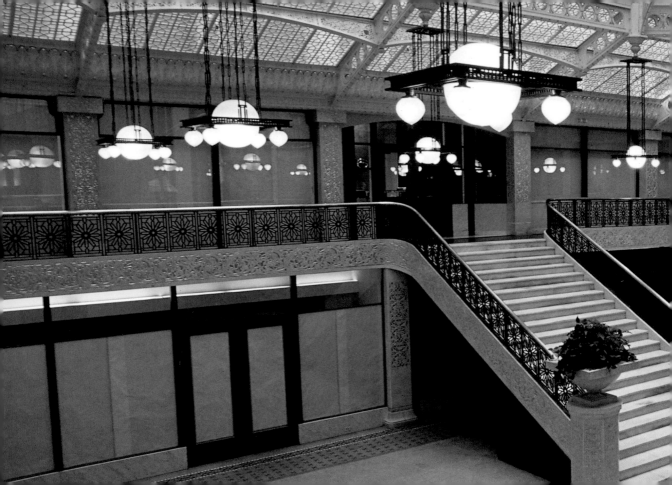

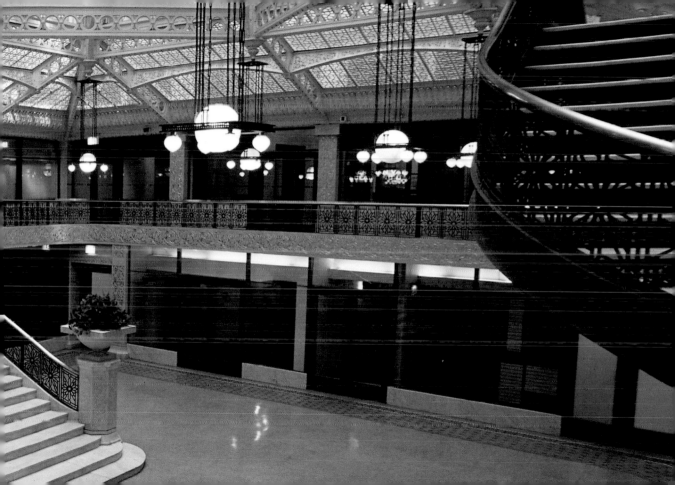

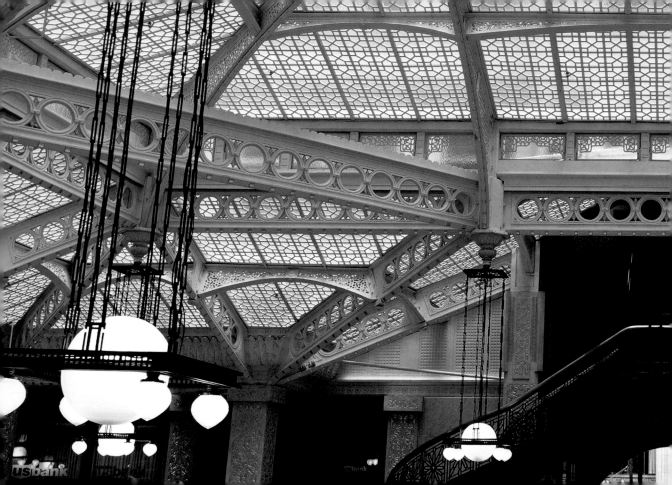

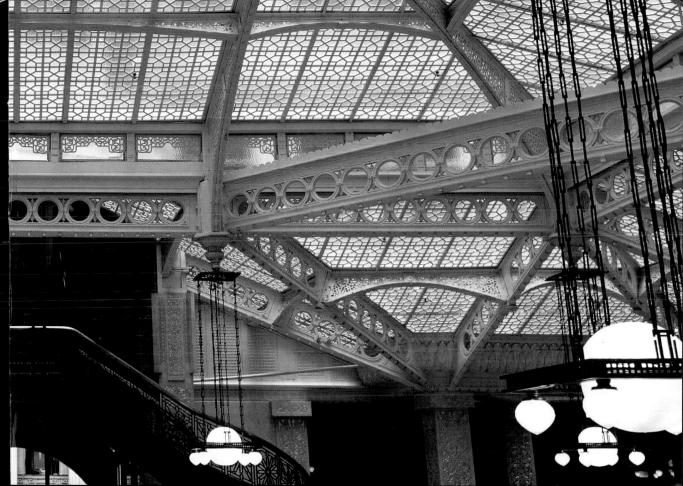

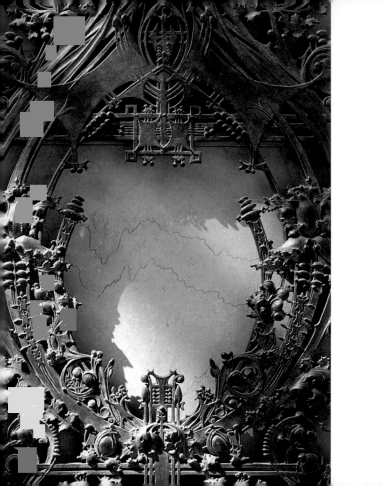

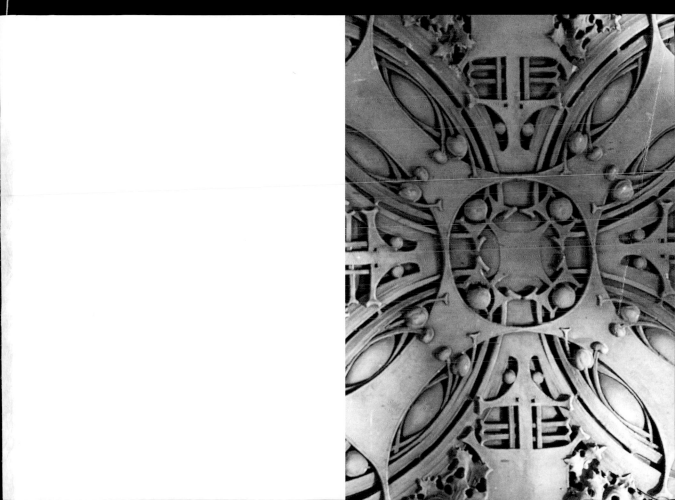

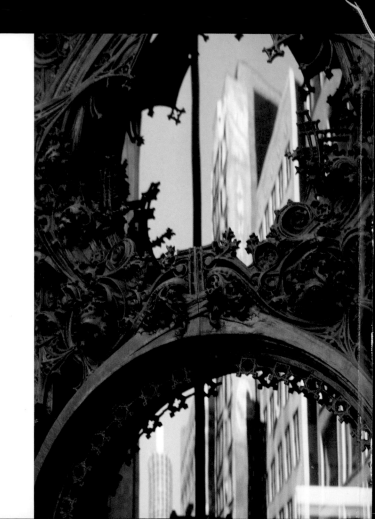

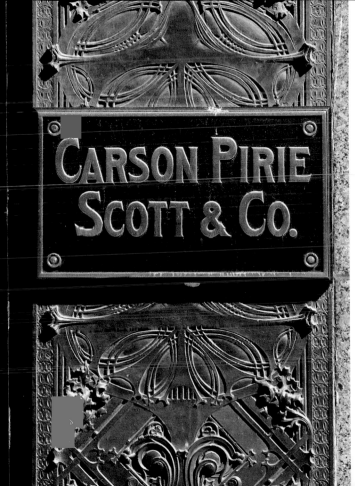

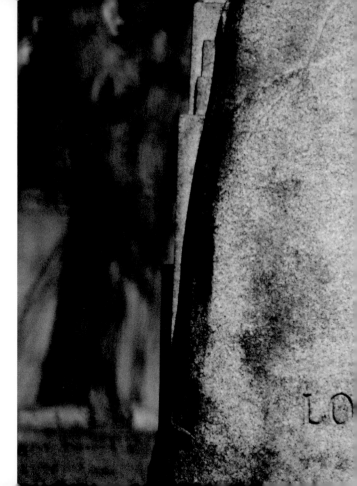

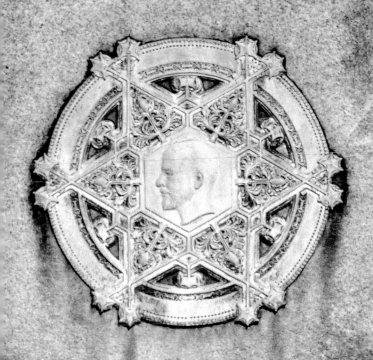

LIS HENRI SULLIVAN

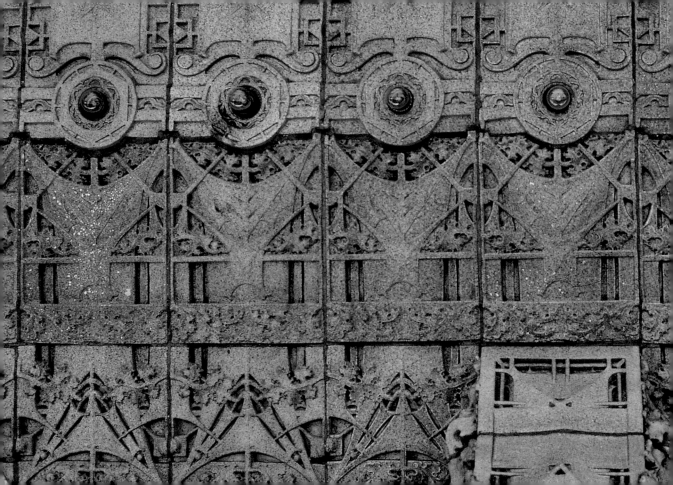

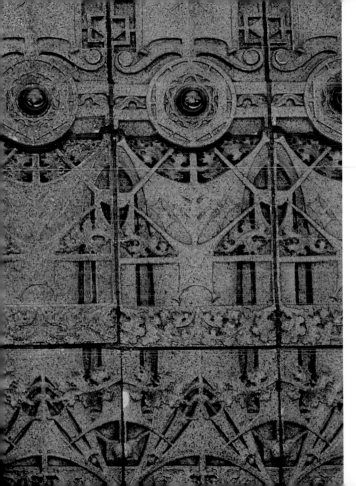

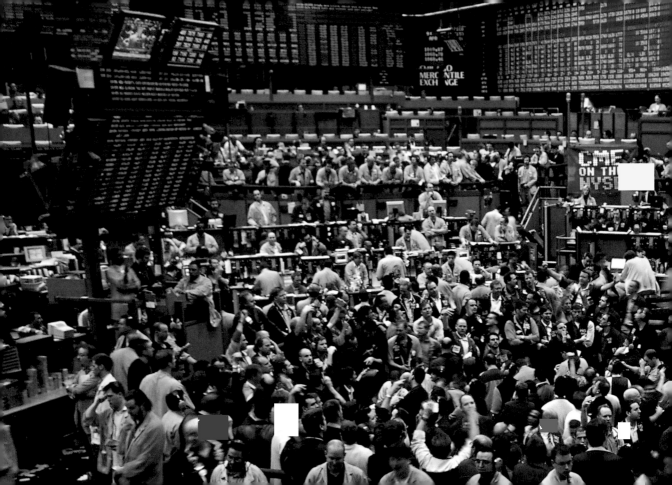

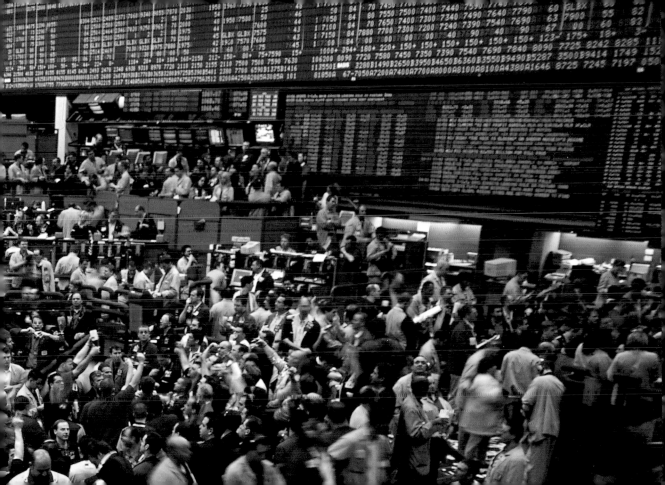

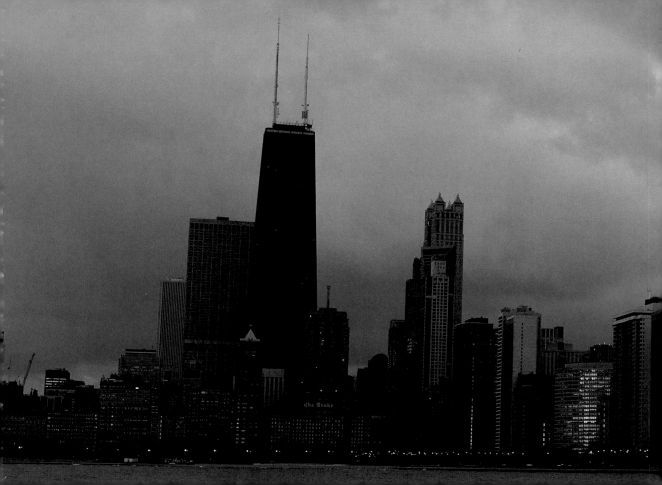

The Drake

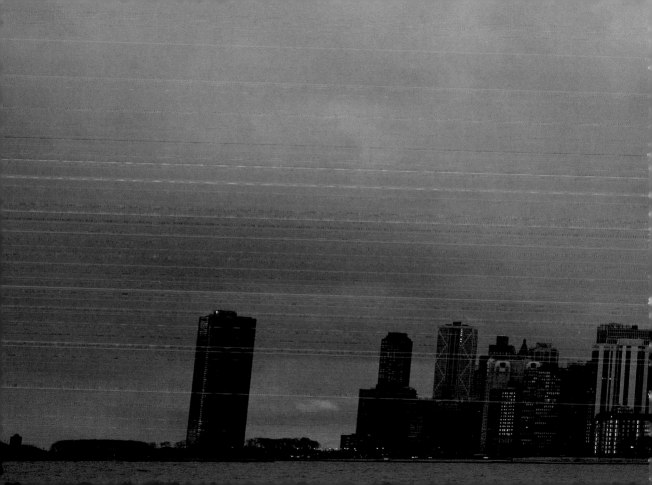

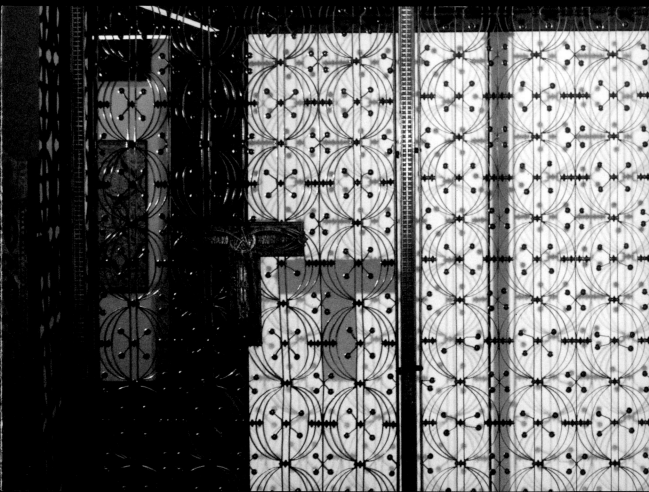

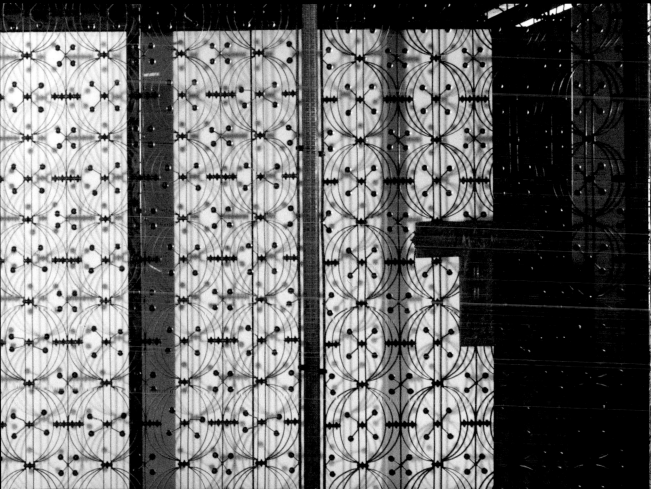

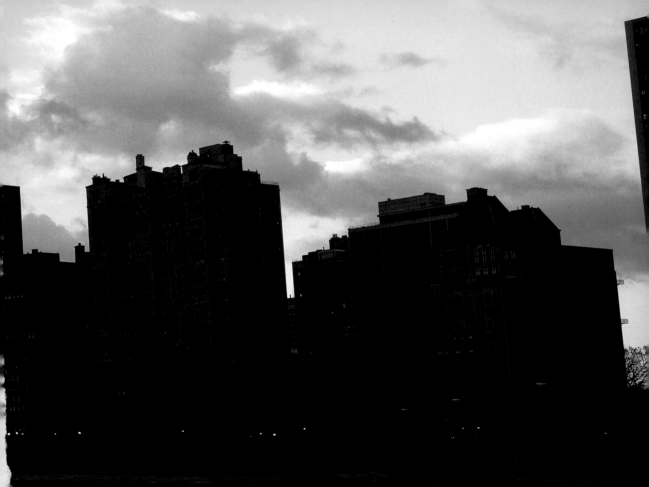

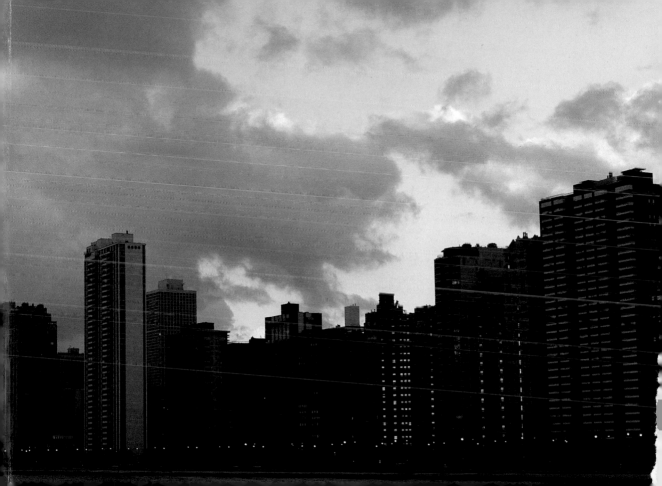

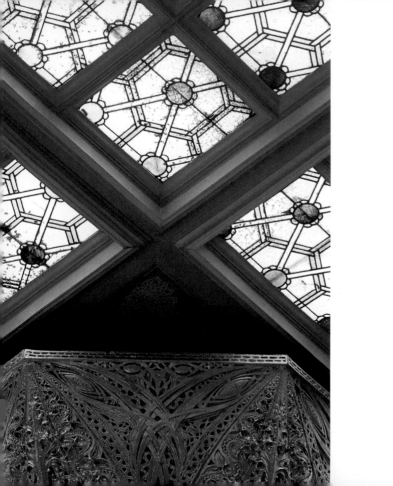

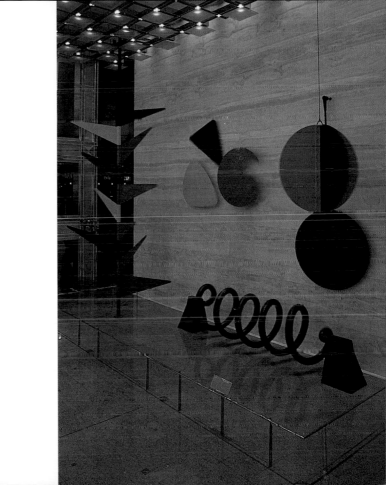

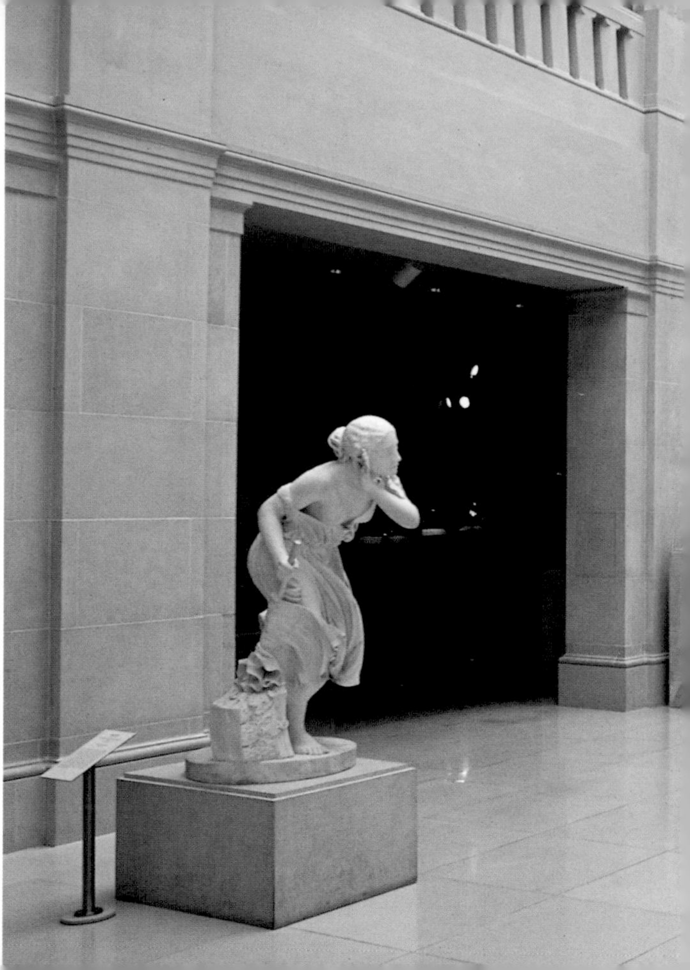

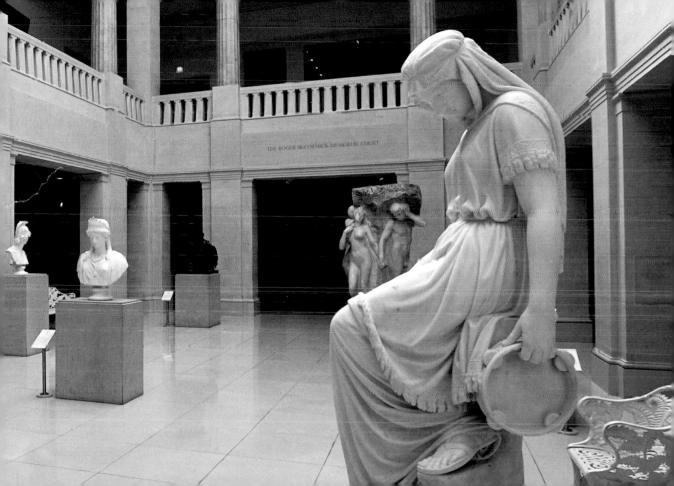

THE ROGER McCORMICK MEMORIAL COURT

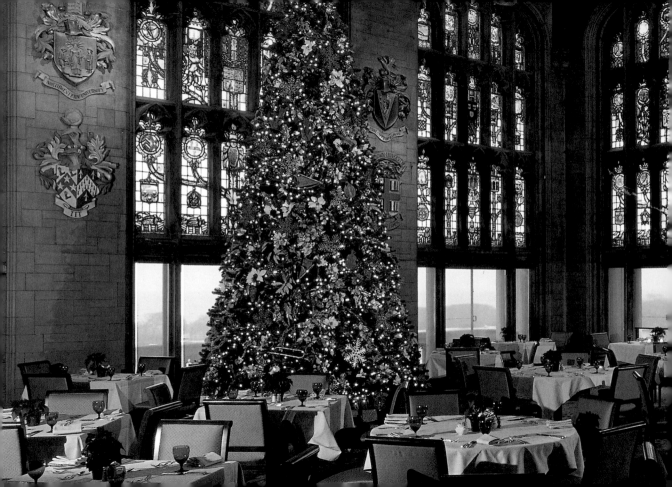

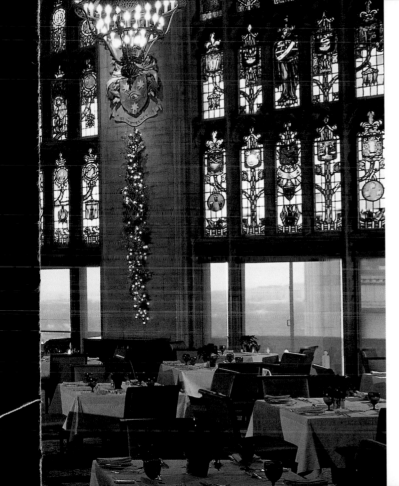

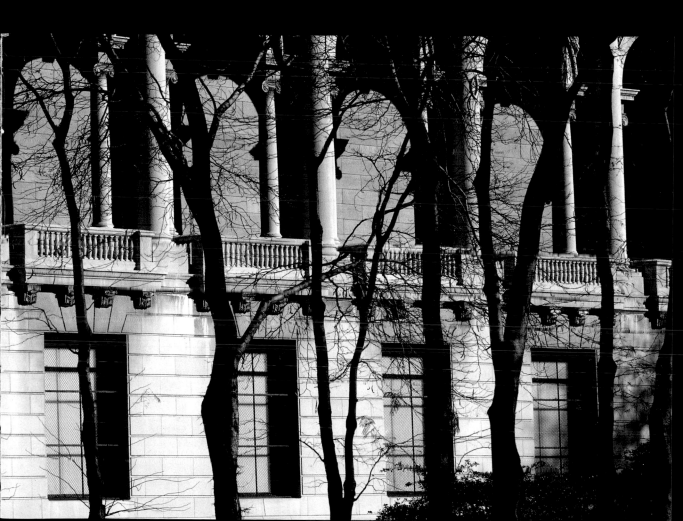

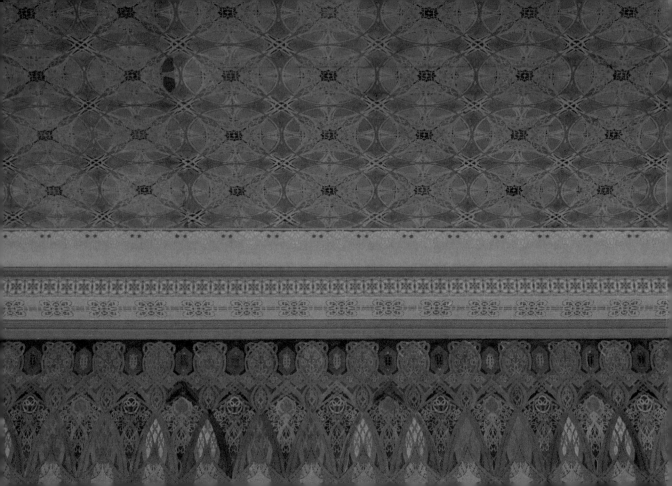

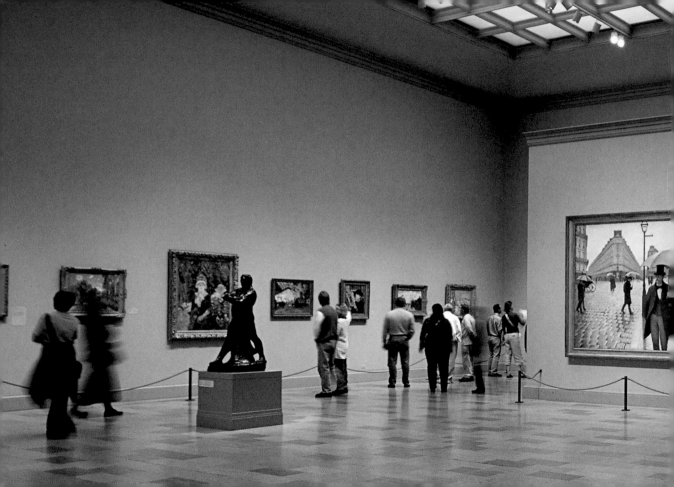

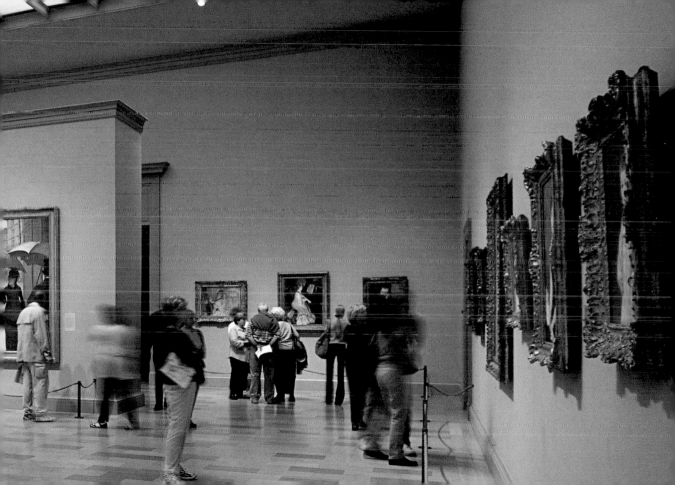

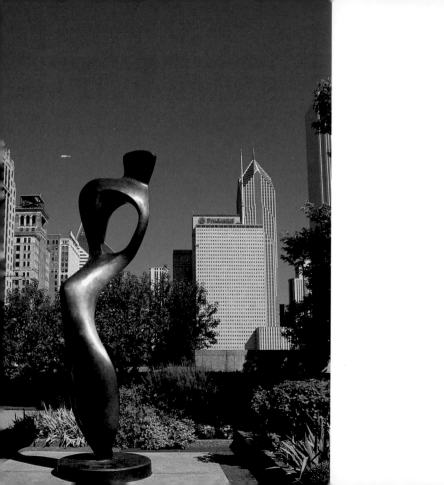

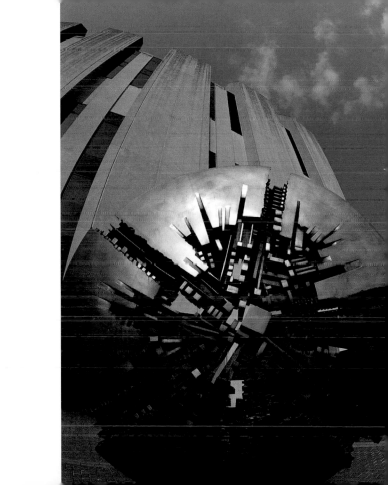

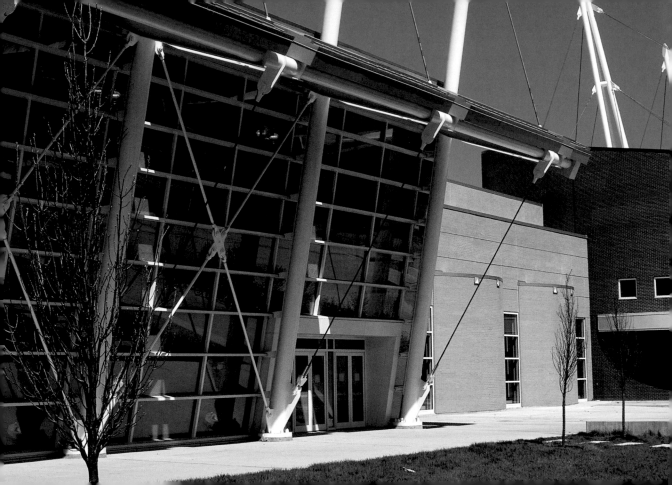

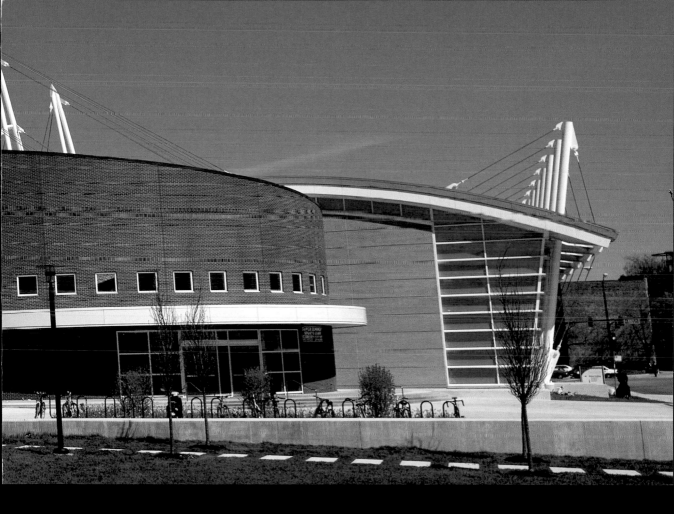

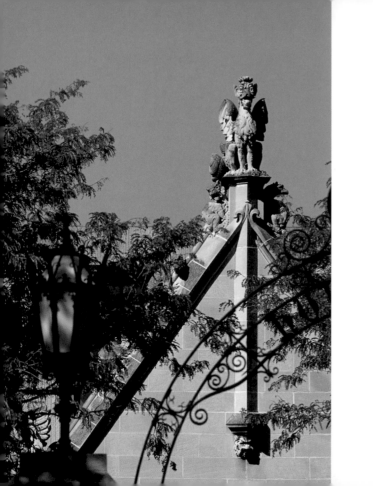

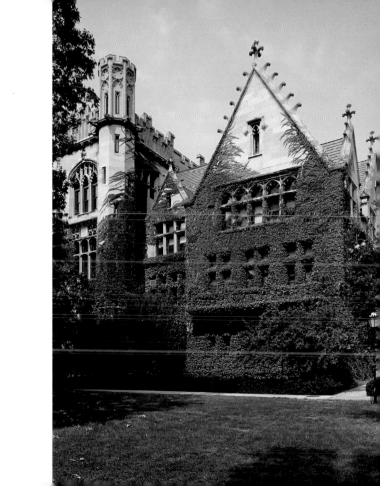

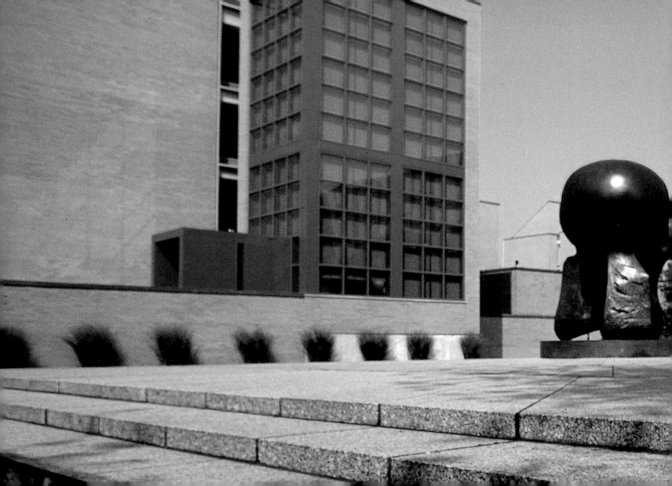

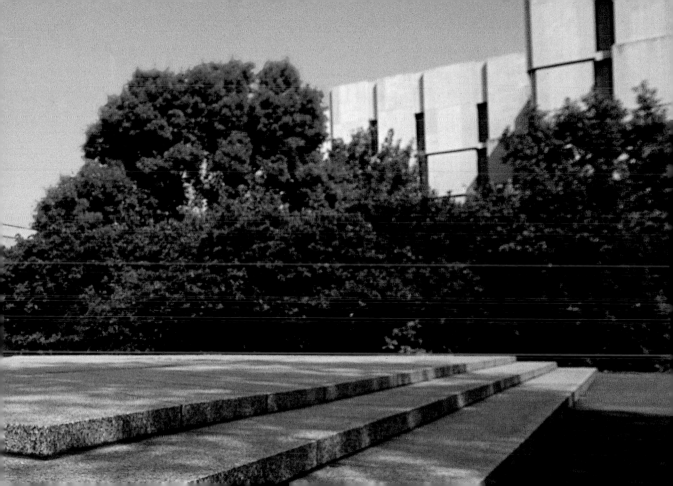

206

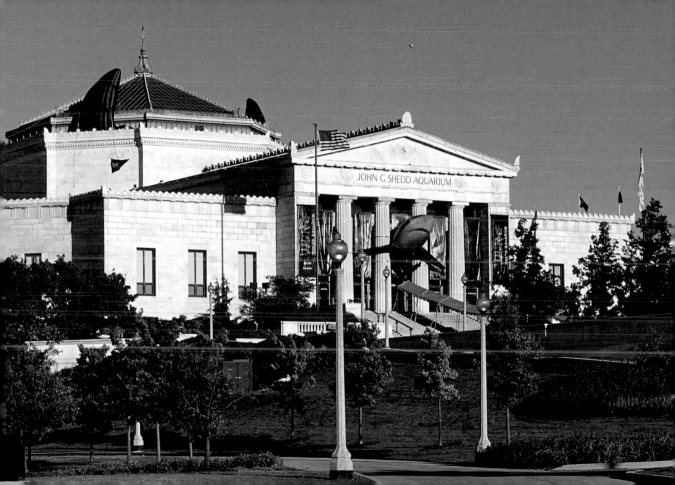

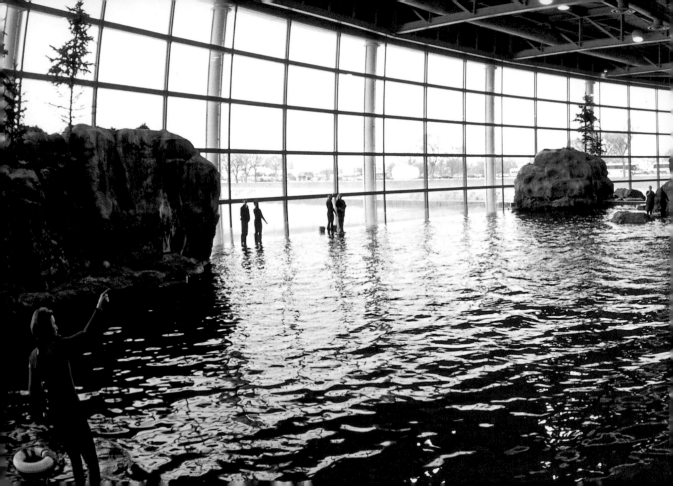

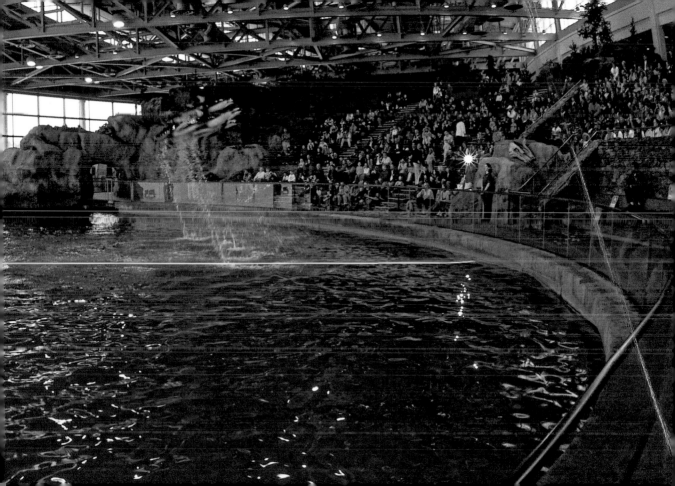

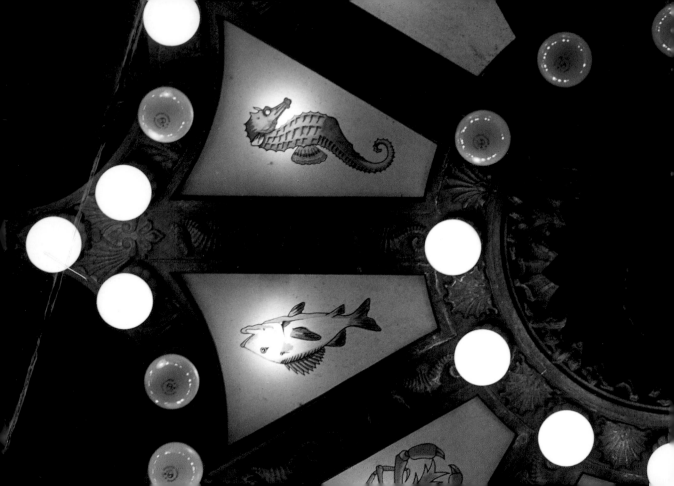

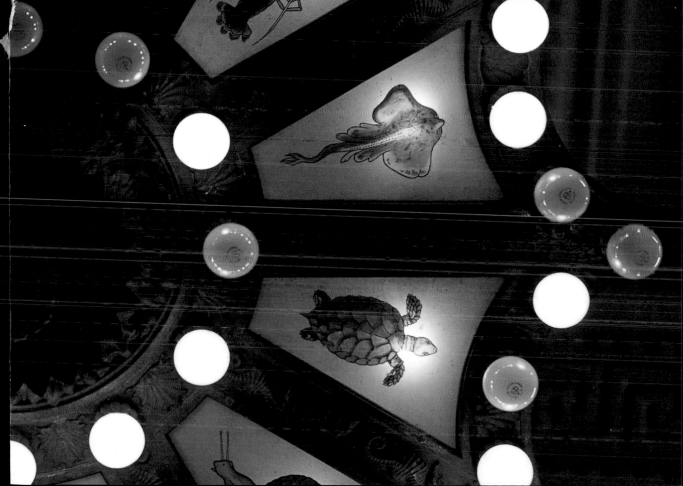

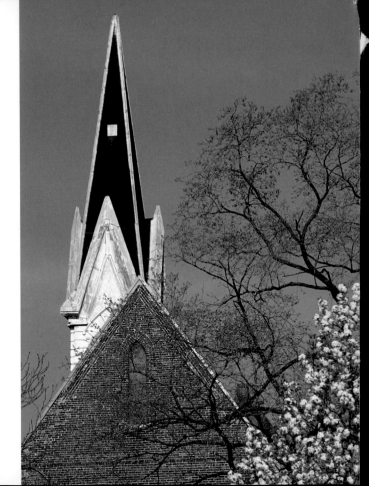

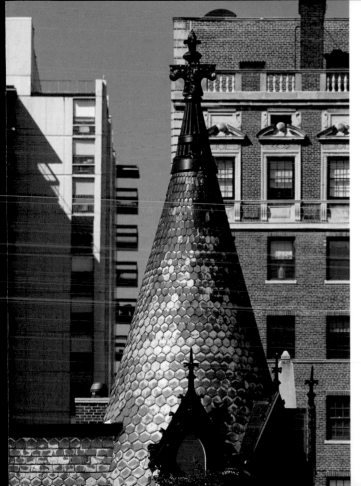

213

214

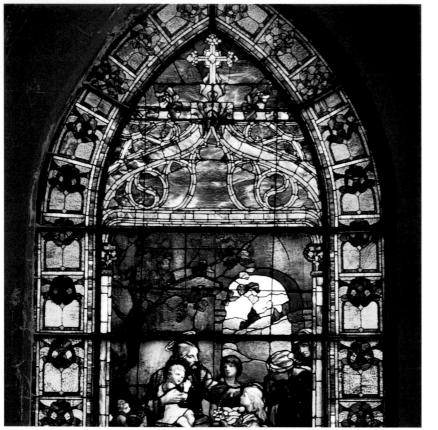

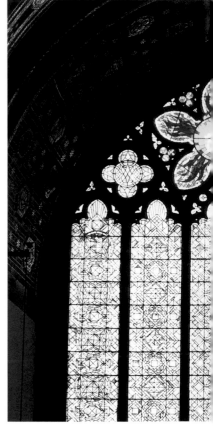

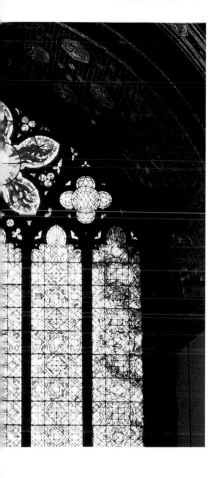

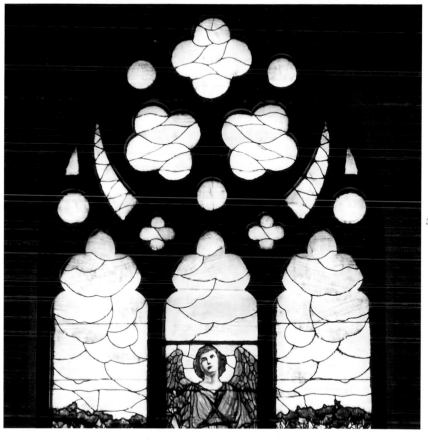

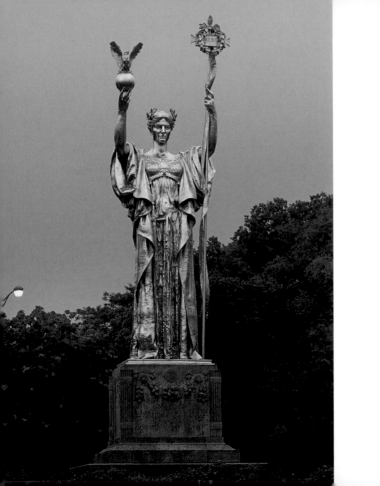

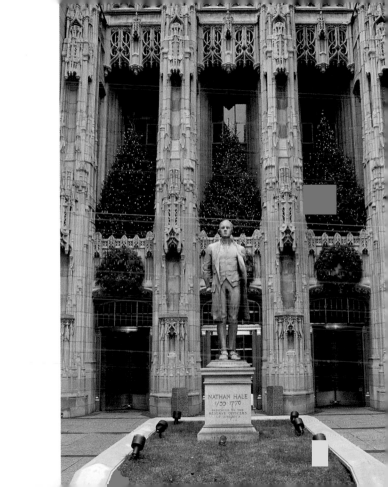

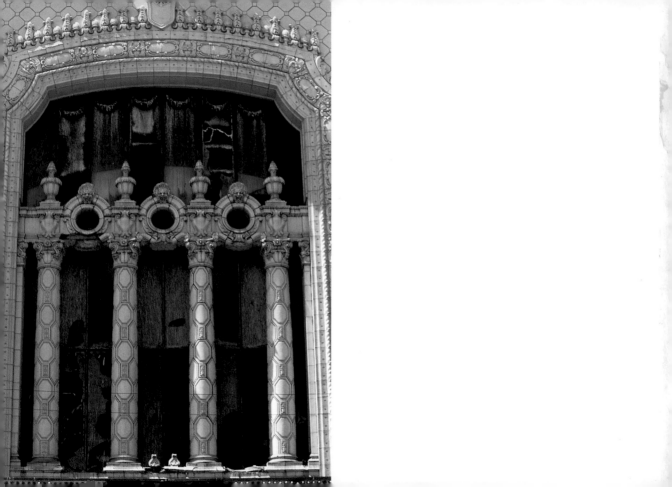

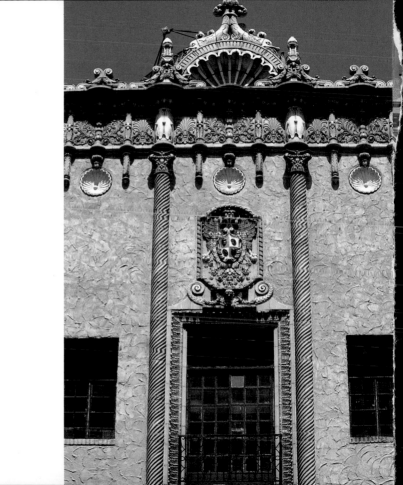

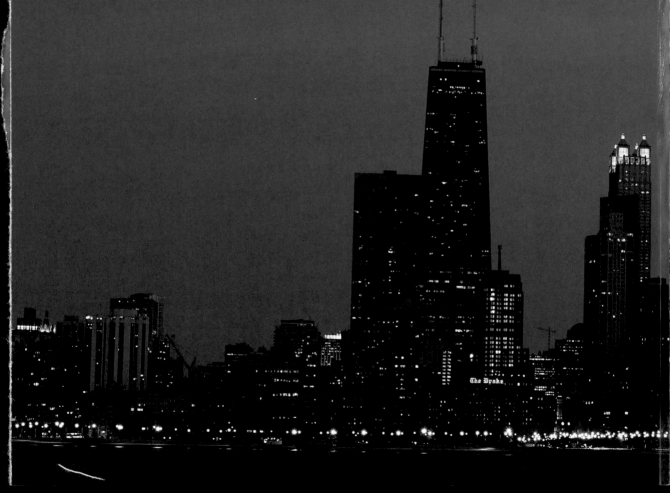

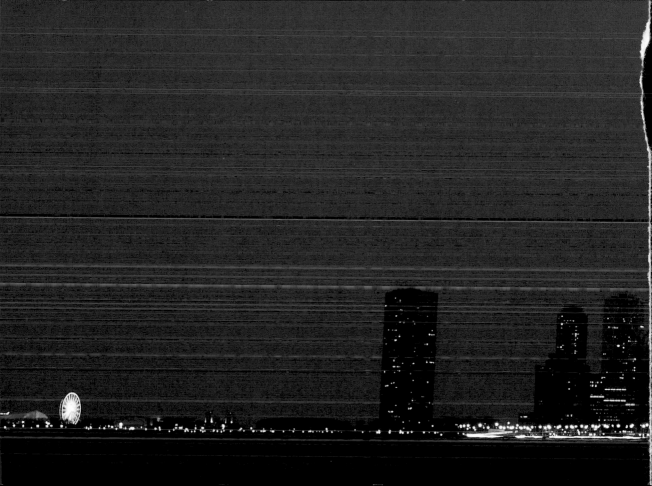

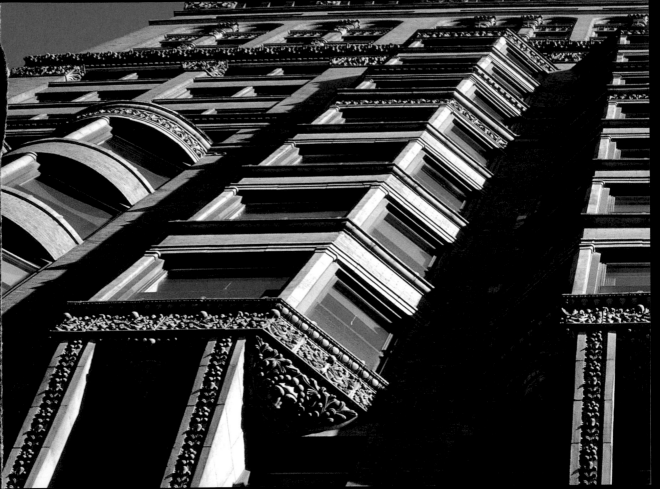

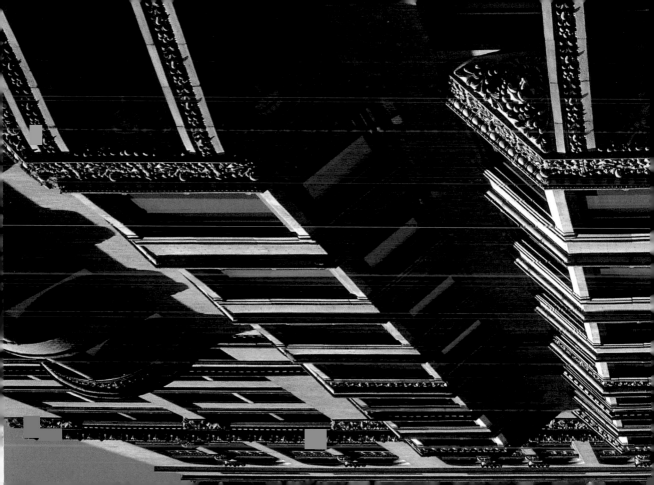

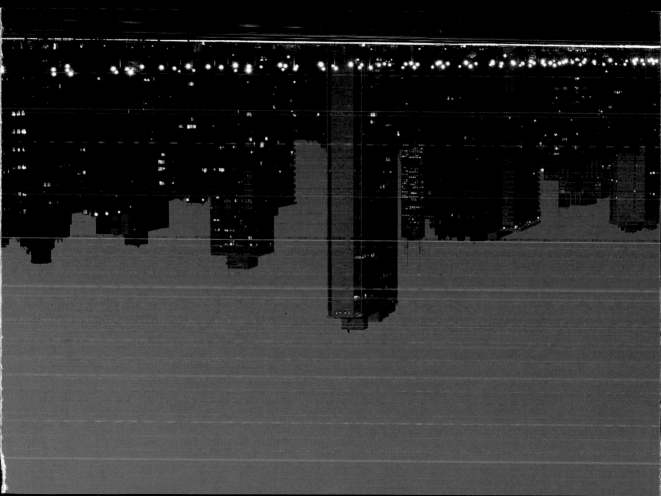

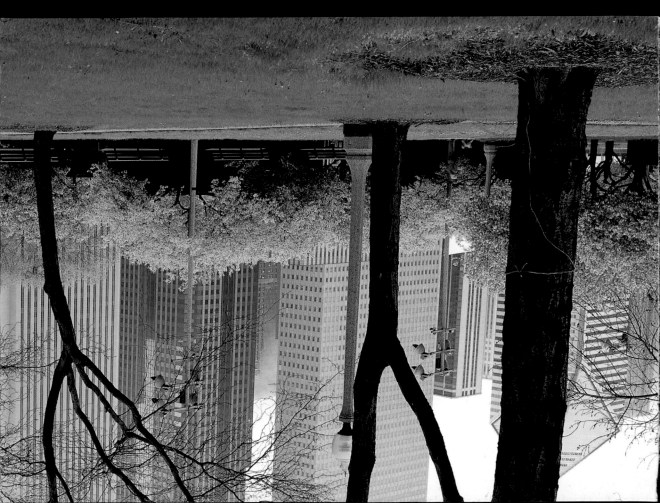

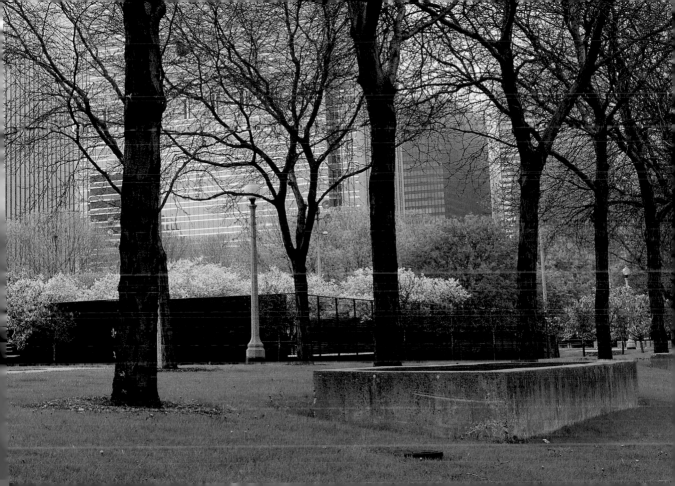

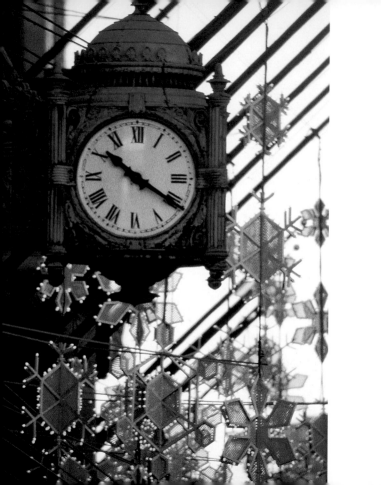

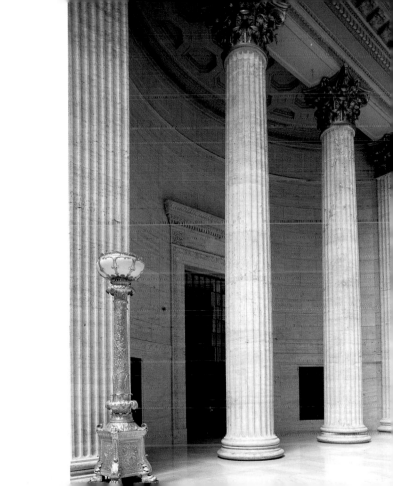

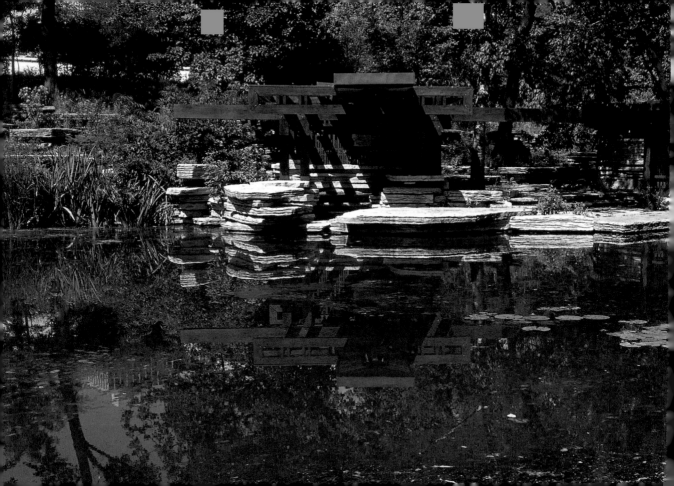

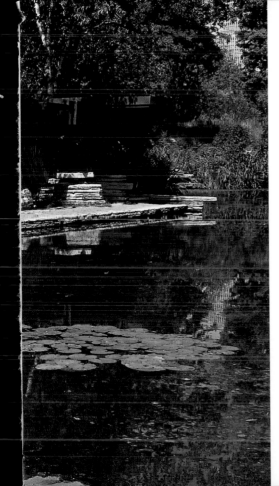

INDEX

PAGES 50 & 55 *Left:* Left to right, Carbide & Carbon Building (1929), 230 North Michigan Avenue, Burnham Brothers architects; AON Building; One Prudential Plaza, *Right:* The clock on Dearborn Station in the historic Printer's Row district

PAGES 51–54 Skyline at dawn, viewed from the Max Adler Planetarium

PAGES 56–57 Ceiling in the lobby of the Ford Theater, once a grand movie palace that opened in 1926 and was designed by George L. and Cornelius W. Rapp for Balaban and Katz. Today it has been gloriously restored and is home to the Best of Broadway presented by Broadway in Chicago.

PAGES 58–59 *Left:* Detail in the lobby of the Ford Theater, *Right:* Foyer of Ford Theater

236

PAGES 60–61 The theater in the Lyric Opera House, which opened in 1929 just six days after the collapse of the stock market; Graham, Anderson, Probst & White, architects

PAGES 62–63 *Left to right:* The Wrigley Building (1921 and 1924); Graham, Anderson & Probst, architects; Batcolumn, (1977), 100-foot-high steel sculpture by Claus Oldenberg; lobby of the Lyric Opera House; Graham, Anderson, Probst & White, architects; the two cylindrical apartment buildings of Marina City (1964); Bertrand Goldberg Associates, architects

PAGES 64–65 Marina City towers reflected on a building at La Salle and Erie streets

PAGES 66–67 *Left:* Portion of skyline with Navy Pier in background; from left, One Prudential Plaza, AON Building *Right:* In foreground, the roof garden of City Hall, landscaped with prairie plants; in background to the left, a portion of the State of Illinois Center

PAGES 68–69 *Left:* The Hotel Sofitel Chicago Water Tower; Jean Paul Viguier, architect, *Right:* The Hotel Sofitel Chicago Water Tower

PAGES 70–71 Interior of the State of Illinois Center (1985); Helmut Jahn, architect

PAGES 72–73 *Left:* 333 Wacker Drive (1983); Kohn, Pedersen, and Fox, architects, *Right:* Lakeshore Drive Apartments (1952); Ludwig Mies Van Der Rohe, architect

PAGES 74–75 Reflections, *Left to right:* AON Building reflected on the façade at the back of the Art Institute; building in Federal Plaza (Dearborn & Adams streets) reflected on building across the street; the Hancock Tower reflected on a building at La Salle and Erie streets

PAGES 76–77 *Left:* Associates Center (1983) on Michigan Avenue, *Right:* Tower of the Chicago Tribune Building (1925) on Michigan Avenue; Raymond Hood & John Mead Howells, architects

PAGES 78–79 Stones from architectural gems around the world are set into the side of the Chicago Tribune Building (1925)

PAGES 80–81 Restored 19th-century townhouses on Schiller Street near Lake Michigan

PAGES 124–25 Dead trees in Grant Park decorated with rubber hoses

PAGES 126–27 Enjoying the late-summer sun at North Street Beach

PAGE 128 North Street Beach at sunset

PAGES 130–31 The spectacular Jay Pritzker Pavilion (2004) in Millennium Park, fashioned of stainless steel, designed by Frank Gehry

PAGES 132–33 The Auditorium Theater (1889), Adler & Sullivan, architects; one of the first public buildings in Chicago to use electric lighting and air conditioning

PAGES 134–35 *Left:* Staircase in the Auditorium Theater (1889), *Right:* Spectacular chandeliers by American glass artist, Dale Chihuly, adorn the ceiling of NoMi Restaurant at the Park Hyatt Hotel on Michigan Avenue

238

PAGES 136–37 Center, the roof of the Harold Washington Library Center

PAGES 138–39 The Harold Washington Library Center, 400 South State Street, designed by Thomas Beeby of Hammond, Beeby, and Babka

PAGES 140–41 The Tiffany Dome in the Chicago Cultural Center (1897), 78 East Washington Street, which served for nearly one hundred years as the central branch of the Chicago Public Library

PAGES 142–43 One of seven aluminum sculptures atop the Harold Washington Library Center

PAGES 144–45 Part of a mural that pays homage to the Chicago School of Architecture (1980) by Richard Haas, 1211 North La Salle Street; left to right, Frank Lloyd Wright, John W. Root, Daniel Burnham, Louis H. Sullivan

PAGE 146 Nathan G. Moore House (1895), 333 North Forest in Oak Park; Frank Lloyd Wright, architect

PAGES 148–49 James Charnley House (1892) at 1365 North Astor St., designed by Frank Lloyd Wright when he was working for Adler & Sullivan

PAGES 150–51 *Left:* Detail of the Walter H. Gale house (1892), 1031 West Chicago Street, Oak Park; Frank Lloyd Wright, architect, *Right:* Boulders, designed and executed by sculptor Richard Bock (c. 1898) on roof of the Frank Lloyd Wright Home and Studio (1889–98); architect, Frank Lloyd Wright in Oak Park

PAGES 152–53 Children's playroom in Frank Lloyd Wright Home and Studio (1889–98) in Oak Park

PAGES 154–55 Portion of the skylight in Frank Lloyd Wright Home and Studio (1889–98) in Oak Park

PAGES 156–57 Downstairs octagonal library where Frank Lloyd Wright received his clients at his Home and Studio in Oak Park

PAGES 158–59 William E. Martin House (1903), 636 Northeast, Oak Park, Frank Lloyd Wright, architect

PAGE 160 Exterior of the Frederick C. Robie House (1910),

PAGES 202–203 *Left:* Lamp post and gargoyle by the gate at the main entrance to the University of Chicago campus, *Right:* Fabled Gothic architecture of Ryerson Hall at the University of Chicago

PAGES 204–205 Statue by Henry Moore (1967), commemorating the first self-sustaining controlled nuclear chain reaction on December 2, 1942, by Enrico Fermi at the University of Chicago. The Max Palevsky residential commons (2001), designed by Ricardo Legorreta, is in the background.

PAGES 206–207 The John G. Shedd Aquarium, (1929); Graham, Anderson, Probst & White, architects

PAGES 208–209 Dolphin Show at the Shedd Aquarium, housed in a 1991 glass extension of the building

240

PAGES 210–11 Chandelier in the lobby of the Shedd Aquarium

PAGES 212–13 *Left:* Tower on La Salle Street Church in Old Town, *Right:* Tower on building at North State Parkway and Schiller street

PAGES 214–15 Windows, left to right: "Christ Blessing the Little Children" by Louis Tiffany in the Second Presbyterian Church on South Michigan; Rockefeller Chapel at the University of Chicago; "Angel in the Lilies" by John La Farge in the Second Presbyterian Church on South Michigan

PAGES 216–17 *Left:* Statue of the Republic (1918), created by sculptor Daniel Chester French, *Right:* Statue of Nathan Hale in front of the Tribune Building on North Michigan Avenue

PAGES 218–19 *Left:* The Uptown Theater on Broadway & Lawrence streets (1925), *Right:* The historic Aragon Ballroom on Lawrence Street near Broadway (1926)

PAGES 220 & 225 Façade of the Manhattan Building (1890), 431 South Dearborn Street, William LeBaron Jenney, architect

PAGES 221–24 Skyline at night from North Street Beach

PAGES 226–27 Skyline viewed from Grant Park

PAGES 228–29 *Left:* the clock on Marshall Field's Department Store at State and Washington streets, *Right:* Marble Corinthian columns in the "Great Hall" at Union Station (1925). Daniel Burnham started the plan and it was completed by the firm of Graham, Anderson, Probst & White.

PAGES 230–31 The Rookery, a 1930s masterpiece of Prairie School landscape architecture in Lincoln Park, restored to its original glory; Alfred Caldwell, designer

PAGES 232–33 Sunrise on Lake Michigan at North Street Beach

COVER *Left:* A bird's-eye view of the Navy Pier and Chicago skyline on a summer evening. This amusement park, located on the lakefront just north of the Chicago River, is a popular destination the year round. *Right:* A spectacular view looking northeast from the ninetieth-floor roof of the Sears Tower